Advance Praise for

Less is More

Here it is! The leading thinkers on simplicity, sustainability and doing more with less, gathered together in an inspiring volume that will have you smiling, nodding and saying "Yes!" in affirmation.

— Ed Begley, Jr., "Living Like Ed"

Our species confronts a triple crisis: every biological system is deteriorating, we face growing social inequality, and the global economy has entered what could be a long depression. In their book, *Less Is More*, Cecile Andrews and Wanda Urbanska give us a blueprint for addressing all three of these crises at the same time. Through their deep understanding of the connection between personal enlightenment and social action, they chart a pathway for saving humanity from itself. Do us all a favor and read this book.

— Dr. Kevin Danaher,
Co-Founder, Global Exchange,
Green Festivals, Global Citizen Center

With our economy and climate in crisis, these times call for a change in how we live. Visionaries Cecile Andrews and Wanda Urbanska show us that living simply is a joyful antidote for these global problems. With words fresh from the minds of visionary leaders, Less is More will help anyone recognize that living simply is a win-win-win: good for the planet, for communities and for your pocket book.

— Alisa Gravitz,
Executive Director of Green America

Simplicity is a wonderful route to the well-being of people and the planet. The writers assembled here are absolutely inspiring, giving you hope and vision. Humanity still has time!

> — Carol Holst, co-director of Simple Living America
> and editor of *Get Satisfied*

Less Is More — in its elegant form and substantive content — communicates the essential message that simplicity is the solution to so many of our problems. This book is a powerful tool for those curious about how to simplify their lives and veteran simplicity advocates alike. A definite must-read!

> — Erik Assadourian, Research Associate, Project Director,
> State of the World 2010, Worldwatch Institute

An impressive collection of essays from wise authors... authors who have known for years that the path to economic stability, environmental restoration and creating vibrant, healthy communities can be found by learning to do more with less. *Less is More* is a must read in these challenging times.

> — Dave Wampler, founder, The Simple Living Network,
> www.simpleliving.net

Andrews and Urbanska have done it again, making a compelling case for why less is better by bringing together an eclectic array of writers, thinkers and sustainabilty advocates who live in ways that echo what they write about. We all know that you can't buy happiness, great friends or a healthy community. By rediscovering the joy and satisfaction that comes from simplicity, frugality, and community, we can remake the world where everyone gets to share. Read the book, then live its lessons.

> — Lisa Kivirist and John Ivanko,
> co-authors of *ECOpreneuring* and *Rural Renaissance*

Less is More

Embracing simplicity
for a healthy planet,
a caring economy and
lasting happiness

Cecile Andrews & Wanda Urbanska

NEW SOCIETY PUBLISHERS

Cataloging in Publication Data:
A catalog record for this publication is available
from the National Library of Canada.

Cover design by Diane McIntosh.
Photo: © iStock/Elena Ray

Printed in Canada.
First printing June 2009.

Paperback ISBN: 978-0-86571-650-6

Inquiries regarding requests to reprint all or part of *Less is More*
should be addressed to New Society Publishers at the address below.

To order directly from the publishers, please call toll-free (North
America) 1-800-567-6772, or order online at www.newsociety.com

Any other inquiries can be directed by mail to:
New Society Publishers
P.O. Box 189, Gabriola Island, BC V0R 1X0, Canada
(250) 247-9737

New Society Publishers' mission is to publish books that contribute
in fundamental ways to building an ecologically sustainable and just
society, and to do so with the least possible impact on the environment,
in a manner that models this vision. We are committed to doing this
not just through education, but through action. This book is one step
toward ending global deforestation and climate change. It is printed on
Forest Stewardship Council-certified acid-free paper that is **100% post-
consumer recycled** (100% old growth forest-free), processed chlorine
free, and printed with vegetable-based, low-VOC inks, with covers
produced using FSC-certified stock. Additionally, New Society purchases
carbon offsets based on an annual audit, operating with a carbon-
neutral footprint. For further information, or to browse our full list of
books and purchase securely, visit our website at: www.newsociety.com

NEW SOCIETY PUBLISHERS
www.newsociety.com

Mixed Sources

Cert no. SW-COC-001271
© 1996 FSC

Dedicated to
Paul, Rebecca, Daniel and
Maggie the Bichon
(the small dog who is always more).

— Cecile Andrews —

〜

This anthology is dedicated to
Ann Belk whose friendship and
steadfast support mean the world to me.

— Wanda Urbanska —

Contents

Part One: Simplicity Defined

Part Two: Solutions

Part Three: Policies

Afterword

Acknowledgments

When I graduated from college in the sixties, I worked with the American Friends Service Community as a community organizer in the South. One of the places I visited changed me forever: Highlander Center. It was a "training center" where Rosa Parks had participated not long before she took her historic action. The theme of Highlander was (and still is) simple: *The wisdom is in the people.* Bring people together to talk, and they will find the answers to the problems facing them. This became my model for social change.

My ideas about Simplicity have come to me this way — learning from the people. So when I say I have hundreds of people to thank, I mean it. For years I've been talking with people about Simplicity in circles and discussion groups. The idea of Simplicity is wonderful because everyone can contribute. No one is an expert. No one needs an advanced degree to contribute.

In addition to all of the people I've met with over the years, there are the authors in this book. Most of them I know, and they are truly wonderful. I feel so grateful to have had them participate in this work.

Helping us all are the people who have founded organizations in the Simplicity movement: Carol Holst in Simple Living America, Dave Wampler in the Simple Living Network and John de Graaf in the Take Back Your Time organization.

And of course the people at New Society Publishers. How wonderful to deal with real people who care about their work and care about you.

And finally, my husband Paul Andrews. How wonderful to spend my life with such a wonderfully supportive person who not only keeps everything going, but laughs at my jokes.

— Cecile Andrews

I would like to acknowledge with deep gratitude the instrumental support of the Everett Foundation of Charlotte, North Carolina, for providing the funding that helped make my work on this book possible. Additionally, I want to thank the following people who are with me in my life — and heart — every day. Each has helped in his or her own way, personally, professionally and spiritually: My trailblazing mother, Marie Olesen Urbanski Whittaker; my remarkable aunts, Ruth Olesen Kelley and Margaret Olesen Corbin Raley; my beloved sister and guiding star, Jane Urbanski Robbins; Pat Gwyn Woltz; Helen "Copey" Hanes; my cherished friends and colleagues, Bonni Brodnick, Liz Brody, Carol Holst, Don Schumacher, Kay Taylor, Ann Vaughn, Ann Williams, Nicholas Bragg, Norman Davies, Linda C. Fuller, Leonard Kniffel, Aldona Wos, Eve Krzyzanowski, Marion McAdoo Goldwasser, Susan Christian Goulding, Susan King, Georgia Jones-Davis, Charlotte Saper, Stan King, Erik Assadourian, Teresa Van Hoy, Roberto Hasfura, Michael & Judy Van Hoy, Robert & Cama Merritt, Bozena Wiercinska, John Wear, Frank Levering, Kathy Treanor and Charlotte Sheedy; and, of course, Cecile Andrews, who dreamed up *Less is More* in the first place and had the good sense to take it to New Society Publishers. Paul Andrews deserves appreciation for his support. Finally, I'd like to thank my son, Henry, who inspires me every day to give everything I've got to make the world a better place.

— Wanda Urbanska

Preface

Less is More. A startling proposition. The authors in this book, who have been writing and thinking about Simplicity for years, will explain. Hearing from these writers and thinkers is tremendously exciting, and you'll find answers to many of the crises we're facing.

First and foremost, Simplicity is a response to the crisis of our planet. The Earth cannot survive our abuse. In our pursuit of *more*, we've used too many resources, severely polluted the planet, and now we're changing the climate, bringing disaster.

The pursuit of *more*, has brought us a broken economy — with greed, corruption and injustice undermining our nation. When we pursue *more*, without limits, the society breaks down.

What's more, research shows that the pursuit of *more*, doesn't even make people happy! Happiness has declined as our affluence has increased.

Less is more, brings well-being to people in many ways.

When Americans use less, the rest of the world suffers less because countries can serve their own peoples' needs. When rich people have less, a middle class thrives, giving everyone a better, safer quality of life.

And finally, *less is more*, brings individual satisfaction. When you have too much, you savor nothing. If you get a new shirt each week, what's special about that? But an occasional new shirt can truly be enjoyed. Ultimately, using less means we turn away from material things to the true source of happiness: caring for other people.

The writers in this book offer profound new insights into an age-old philosophy. Throughout history, mainstream religions and wisdom traditions have understood the importance of Simplicity, but most people have failed to grasp it. Now our problems are forcing us to consider it.

What is Simplicity? Simplicity is a complex concept, but at the core is voluntary limitation of our outer wealth so that we can have greater inner wealth. Research, history and personal experience show that you can't pursue both at the same time. The belief that being rich will make you happy is simply wrong, yet it continues to hold us captive.

What do people involved in the Simplicity movement do? Usually, people have focused on individual actions: reducing spending so they can work less and have more time for the things that are important to them. Thus, a life with less — less work, less stuff, less clutter — becomes more: more time for friends, family, community, creativity, civic involvement. Less stress brings more fulfillment and joy. Less rushing brings more satisfaction and balance. Less debt brings more serenity. *Less is more.*

But individual change is not enough — it's necessary, but not sufficient. We must create a movement that leads to policy changes. We need policies regulating corporate behavior, work hours, the wealth gap and sustainability. Government must protect and empower, as Berkeley professor George Lakoff says.

But ultimately, Simplicity is no longer just a quaint philosophy for the few. Boston University professor Andrew Bacevich argues that Americans are now in a "crisis of profligacy." In his book *The Limits of Power: The End of American Exceptionalism*, he shows that America's consumerism — our belief that we can have anything we want, with no limits — is destroying our nation. First, our identity as Americans is diminished: "If one were to choose a single word to characterize that identity, it would have to be *more*. For the majority of contemporary Americans, the essence of life, liberty and the pursuit of happiness centers on a relentless personal quest to acquire, to consume, to indulge and to shed whatever constraints might interfere with those endeavors."

We have prided ourselves on being a country that stands for the ideal of freedom. But that, too has been warped. Bacevich warned: "For the United States the pursuit of freedom, as defined in an age of consumerism, has induced a condition of dependence — on imported goods, on imported oil and on credit. The chief desire of the American people, whether they admit it or not, is that nothing should disrupt their access to those goods, that oil, and that credit."

This attitude has led us into acceptance of "war without end" because we cannot continue in our consumerism unless we control oil — indeed, control the world. But as everyone can see, the United States' path has led to failure. We can no longer have what we want or do what we want.

Thus, Americans as a whole must grapple with the idea that "less is more." They must come to understand the idea that living more simply will bring great rewards to themselves, to our country and to the world.

Ultimately, we must change our belief system: Americans believe that "you're on your own," "every man for himself." With this belief comes a cutthroat, irresponsible, uncaring society. But we're beginning to understand that we will survive only if we come to believe that we're *all in this together*, that we need each other. Embracing Simplicity is part of that transformation.

We'll explore this transformation in four parts. First, *definitions*. We'll define "Simplicity" more fully and see how fascinating this complex concept is. Every one of these authors sheds a different light on it.

Then we'll look at concrete *solutions*. What are people doing? It's fascinating to see how people are living more simply — cutting back on their expenditures, their use of energy, the time-wasters in their lives. In particular, it's exciting to see how the emerging community "localization" movement is bringing a new energy and vision to Simplicity.

Next, we'll explore the *policies* we need for a culture of Simplicity. In particular, we'll look at policies for reducing the wealth gap and cutting back on work hours.

Finally, we'll explore what's needed for lasting change. It's not enough to use compact fluorescent bulbs, buy organic foods or drive a Prius — we need a social revolution. And getting involved in this revolution may be one of the most fulfilling things you can do. What do we need to do? It's time to talk. We must revitalize dialogue and democracy. Use this book! Use it to start study groups and workplace discussions. Talking together brings you together.

So we'll explore Simplicity from several angles. As you'll see, there's overlap in all the essays because Simplicity touches all of life. When you make a change in one area, you make changes in others. If you start to walk more, for instance, you help the planet by reducing car emissions, save money on gas, get to know your neighbors and, of course, become a lot healthier!

The authors have been involved in Simplicity issues for a long time. A lot of us have come to know each other over the years, and we've inspired each other. So we can say, without hesitation, that one of the benefits of being involved in this movement is that the people are really, really nice! We love these writers, not just because of what they have to say, but because they are wonderful, charming and, often, funny people.

Of course, all of us have been inspired by one man, and his words can best set the tone for this work.

Thoreau tells a story that captures the essence of what we're talking about. In *Walden* he writes of

> a strong and beautiful bug which came out of the dry leaf of an old table of apple-tree wood, which had stood in a farmer's kitchen for sixty years...from an egg deposited in the living tree many years earlier still...which was heard gnawing out for several weeks, hatched perchance by the heat of an urn. Who does not feel his faith in a resurrection and immortality strengthened by hearing of this? Who knows what beautiful and winged life, whose egg has been buried for ages under many concentric layers of woodenness in the dead dry life of society...may unexpectedly come forth...to enjoy its perfect summer life at last!

Reading these words, we can't help but feel that the idea of Simplicity may, like the beautiful bug, be emerging at this time.

— Cecile and Wanda

PART ONE

Simplicity Defined

Introduction

by Cecile Andrews

I am grateful for what I am and have. My thanksgiving is perpetual. It is surprising how contented one can be with nothing definite — only a sense of existence. My breath is sweet to me. O how I laugh when I think of my vague indefinite riches. No run on my bank can drain it, for my wealth is not possession but enjoyment.

If the day and the night are such that you greet them with joy, and life emits a fragrance like flowers and sweet smelling herbs — is more elastic, starry, and immortal— that is your success.

— HENRY DAVID THOREAU

What Is Simplicity?

I've never tired of this question! Defining "simplicity" is a fascinating and lifelong project. Each one of our authors approaches it differently, showing the incredible depth and complexity of the idea of Simplicity.

Essentially, Simplicity is about creating a life you love, a life that brings you joy and peace of mind or, as Thoreau would say, a life that "emits a fragrance like flowers and sweet smelling herbs: is more elastic, starry, and immortal."

Simplicity allows us to say with Thoreau, "I am grateful for what I am and have, my thanksgiving is perpetual."

People are intuitively drawn to Simplicity, sensing its promise of the re-enchantment of life. But at the same time, they fear it, worrying that they will never enjoy themselves again. But they're mistaken — if you're not laughing and smiling more as you simplify, you're not doing it right.

Most people see Simplicity as being only about frugality, and while that's a key element, it's something much wider. Simplicity is a lens through which to view all of life.

To explain what I mean, let's step back a minute and look at some basic dictionary definitions of "simplicity":

Absence of luxury, pretentiousness, ornament, etc.; plainness: a life of simplicity.

Freedom from deceit or guile; sincerity; artlessness; naturalness: a simplicity of manner.

Freedom from artificial ornament, pretentious style, or luxury; plainness; as, simplicity of dress, of style, or of language; simplicity of diet; simplicity of life.

Freedom from subtlety or abstruseness; clearness; as, the simplicity of a doctrine; the simplicity of an explanation or a demonstration.

Plainness, clarity, clearness — what these definitions have in common is a sense of clearing away the extraneous, stripping away the inessential. It's about what's real, what's important or, again, as Thoreau put it, "life near the bone where it is sweetest."

So Simplicity is about much more than ten tips to save money. Ultimately, Simplicity is asking yourself: "How do I really want to live? What truly makes me happy? What are my actions doing to the planet? How does my lifestyle contribute to the greater good? Ultimately Simplicity is about knowing who you are, being clear about your values, understanding what brings true well-being. It's cutting through the commercial static of manipulation and deceit that says that the consumer society is the good life. Ultimately, it's about taking time to think and finding clarity; it's about discernment and deliberation.

In particular, it's about seeing clearly — seeing the consumer society for what it is. One person who sees clearly is the Dalai Lama. In his book *Ethics for the New Millennium*, he comments on his experience as an outsider coming to our culture: "Those living in the materially developed countries, for all their industry, are in some ways less satisfied, are less happy, and to some extent suffer more than those living in the least developed countries."

He sees that our values have been distorted:

> [The rich] are so caught up with the idea of acquiring still more that they make no room for anything else in their lives. In their absorption, they actually lose the dream of happiness, which riches were to have provided. As a result, they are constantly tormented, torn between doubt about what might happen and the hope of gaining more, and plagued with mental and emotional suffering...so many feel uneasy and dissatisfied with their lives. They experience feelings of isolation; then follows depression.

His diagnosis of our problem? A theme all of our writers echo — our lack of connection with each other. He finds that "in place of our dependence on one another for support, today, wherever possible, we tend to rely on machines and services. We find modern living organized so that it demands the least possible direct dependence on others.... we find a high degree of loneliness and alienation."

What we'll find our authors saying is that we're happier and more fulfilled when we limit our outer riches and focus on inner riches. It's not about impoverishment — where people do not have enough — particularly enough food, or shelter or safety. It's about everyone having enough. Simplicity is about having enough, but not too much. Affluence, as the Dali Lama notes, brings inner, spiritual impoverishment.

But of course we also have physical impoverishment in our society. Is Simplicity relevant to the poor? Yes, but in a different way. The Simplicity movement is a middle-class movement because it concerns making a choice about how to live, and the poor have few choices. Instead of cutting back their spending, the poor need more money to spend. The poor need new policies rather than Simplicity tips. They need policies that support higher minimum wages, good jobs, affordable housing and health care — policies that make it possible for the poor to live simply.

Simplicity is relevant to the poor in another way — it challenges our beliefs about money: As long as we allow unbridled profit to be our primary goal, people, and particularly corporations, will lie, cheat and treat workers unfairly. Ultimately, profit is the reason we go to war, and it's the poor who fight these wars. As Americans use up more than their share of resources, others have less. As Americans force other nations to cater to their needs, poor countries neglect their own citizens. As Americans insist on pursuing "more," they destroy the planet for the rest of humankind. Americans must learn to "live simply so that others may simply live," as Elizabeth Seton (1774–1821), the first American-born saint, said.

Simplicity, then, is about taking control over your life and resisting the forces of the dominant society that tell us to claw our way to the top, to be a winner, regardless of consequences. Being a winner does not necessarily make you happy! And in fact, it most likely won't. Again, as Thoreau says, success is when you feel contented "with only a sense of existence."

Enjoy the many paths to Simplicity our writers explore.

Simple Living: Lessons from the World of Television

by Wanda Urbanska

WANDA URBANSKA leads the simple life in Mount Airy, North Carolina, where she raises her 12-year-old son, Henry, and is active in community life. She is the author or co-author of seven books, including *Simple Living, Moving to a Small Town* and *Nothing's Too Small to Make a Difference*. A graduate of Harvard University, Wanda is the host-producer of *Simple Living with Wanda Urbanska* (simplelivingtv.net), a nationally syndicated public television series that has produced four broadcast seasons of programming. She is a speaker, blogger and sustainability life coach and has been published in the *Washington Post, Los Angeles Times, Chicago Tribune, American Libraries, Mother Earth News, Natural Home, Rotarian, Vogue* and many other newspapers and magazines.

WHEN I SET OUT to create the *Simple Living with Wanda Urbanska* public television series back in 2000, my aim was to present a magazine-style program exploring the attractions of pared-down, eco-friendly living. The target audience: middle America.

The strategy, developed in partnership with writer/ director Frank Levering, was to draw viewers with the honey of a slower pace, served with a salubrious side of community life and some flavorful, locally grown slow food. Viewers, we were convinced, would be called to change hearts, minds and habits when presented with a vision of life as it could and should be — rather than guilted into change by finger-wagging and images of environmental degradation and calamity. So we beat the drum for change, albeit softly, and with a twinkle in our eyes. Or *my* eyes, I should say, since I was the front woman, the TV host, chief cook, bottle washer and all-important fundraiser.

Simple Living's four tenets — environmental steward-ship, thoughtful consumption, community involvement and financial responsibility — were presented overtly and subliminally throughout each of the show's 39 episodes, along with the mantra, "Nothing's too small to make a difference." Picking up a trash-bound paperclip, repurposing your mother's 1960s skirt into kitchen curtains, installing a water-saving, dual-flush commode; each of these action steps qualified.

Non-partisan, the series was enjoyed (and supported) by Republicans and Democrats, Christians and atheists, men and women, people of all ages, races and tax brackets. What little heat we took invariably came from within our own camp. I'll never forget one colleague upbraiding me for the show's premise. He said it placed too much pressure on individual action at the expense of what he viewed as the more salient issue of public policy. Only problem, the *Simple Living* franchise was charged with producing a how-to lifestyle series — not public affairs programming — as we were reminded by our public television distribution partners whenever our content strayed from its core mission.

At the heart of our series was its quirky sensibility, teaching by example. We tried to hold up a picture of American life — often using actual picture frames — to let viewers decide for themselves if they would choose the easy, prefab culture of convenience, disposability and fast living or would prefer another version.

Once, for a show on overcoming overload, we conducted what used to be called man-on-the-street interviews at the Thruway Shopping Center in Winston-Salem, North Carolina. The questions were about time. Did people have enough of it? Were they more time-pressured today than in the past?

Our results were telling…and chilling.

On that summer day in 2006, no one had time to talk — or almost no one. As I approached him — microphone in hand — one middle-aged man was caught moving briskly from the parking lot toward Border's Books. Racking his brain to come up with an excuse, he looked desperate.

"Sorry," he said lamely, "I'm from out of town."

"Where?" I countered.

"North Carolina," he said.

"That's good," I responded, trying to engage. But, by then, he had vanished.

As a print reporter in Los Angeles in the 1980s, I recall similar random woman-in-the-mall interviews, in which people jockeyed for my attention, for a chance to have their say, for their 15 seconds of fame. But for that *Simple Living* segment on time, time pressure had gained the upper hand.

Throughout the series, we did some good-natured fun-poking at the American way of buying — the way so many Americans seem programmed to shop for the newest, the latest, even if the one they have still works — or to shop even if they need nothing at all. We created a recurring feature called "The Thing That Refused to Die" that high-lighted items that were still in use, past the date of planned obsolescence.

For our first show, we shot a still-operational 1923 cash register at the Palace Barber Shop in my hometown of Mount Airy, North Carolina, a.k.a. Simple Living head-quarters. (Our own workspace was an "Office That Refused to Die," a $200-a-month suite once occupied by a dentist, abutting a second-floor beauty parlor patronized by blue-haired ladies who took on average 27 minutes to climb the flight of stairs, but that's another story.) The cash register's owner told me he'd turned down many a swap offer for a new, electronic register. Why trade, he reasoned, when his old Nelly never broke down, worked during power out-ages and needed only the occasional oiling. A long line of "Things" followed, among them, a 1920s Model T; an outfit purchased in 1960, still worn by its owner almost five de-cades later; and a 1930s fireboat retired by the New York City Fire Department, which, when pressed into service to fight fires at the World Trade Center after 9/11, still worked.

We tackled larger subjects, too, such as global warming, water conservation, open space preservation, mass transit and green building. We examined the benefits of plant-centered diets and of having *fewer* options; we took on noise pollution and sleep disorders and laid out the many perks of engaging in community life. We advocated for local econo-mies, local food and service education. We showed how to start a Simplicity Circle, made the case for connecting with your elders and invited viewers to simplify their lives so that they could make time to trace their roots.

We traveled the nation and world in search of eco-exemplars, such as Denmark's North Sea island of Samso, an international model for energy self-sufficiency through its solar, wind and renewable energy sources. We carted our cameras into the depths of the Wieliczka Salt Mine, a 900-year-old "Business That Refused to Die" near Krakow, Poland, which had been in continuous operation since 1104. Could Wieliczka be, we wondered, the oldest continuously running business in the world? (Alas, since our 2004 shoot, the salt-mining operation has closed, but the mine's subterranean labyrinth of passages, chambers and medieval sculptures — even chandeliers carved from rock salt — remain a world-class tourist destination.)

We traversed the Flying D Ranch outside Bozeman, Montana, one freezing February morning with Beau Turner to document his family's commitment to bringing Great Plains bison back from the brink of extinction. I traveled to Wayland, Massachusetts, to shoot a church's "Roll or Stroll for Your Soul" Sunday, in which congregants rode bikes, walked or carpooled to service, an eco-celebration that was capped off by the minister's mystical "blessing of the bikes."

We talked to big-city mayors about the benefits of barter and asked whether their cities aspired to be "simple living" meccas. We cast a spotlight on the renaissance of the downtowns of Springfield, Missouri, and Greensboro, North Carolina — the latter catalyzed by the recent opening of a 1.9-acre green space called Center City Park, whose design had been largely shaped by community input. We profiled one-car families and car-share programs and, in Austin, Texas, featured the Plug-In Partners National Campaign, which promotes the development of the plug-in hybrid electric vehicle.

We touted the benefits of buying in bulk, using cloth napkins, rags and reusable bags and reducing one's personal waste stream. We even documented the green remodel of my own mid-century brick ranch house in Mount Airy, celebrating such energy-saving upgrades as double-paned, low-e windows, spray-foam and formaldehyde-free insulation and an indoor drying rack and an outdoor clothesline.

There was no higher high-five moment at our *Simple Living* office, though, than when we got word that we had landed an exclusive interview with President and Mrs. Jimmy Carter. Carter has long been an icon for sustainability advocates like me for his pioneering energy policies and for his steadfast commitment to simple living before, during and after the White House. He might not give us how-to tips, but he surely would deliver inspiration to the eco-faithful.

Our cameras tracked the action over the course of a special donor weekend in April 2005 as supporters from around the world gathered in Atlanta for a briefing on the state of Carter Center work and were later treated to a tour by the Carters of their hometown of Plains, Georgia. There we took the short train ride from downtown Plains out to Jimmy's boyhood home and later do-si-doed at an old-fashioned square dance in town. The term "good sport" comes to mind when recalling both Carters throughout the weekend and subsequent sit-down interview, but especially the stoical Rosalynn Carter, who soldiered on, despite having broken her left wrist just days before.

More than anyone I encountered in the course of the series — or during my 35-year journalism career, for that matter — President Carter stands tall. A dedicated simple liver, a man who has walked the talk his entire life (and did so, literally, down Pennsylvania Avenue for his inauguration in January 1977), Carter doubtless paid for his unassuming frugality politically when he came to Washington and went about challenging the systemic privilege of the place.

A dedicated populist, Carter believed that the first family should set an example for the nation and live by it. To combat the energy crisis, he donned a sweater and turned down the thermostat at the White House. Within the first 100 days of his presidency, Carter targeted energy independence as a national priority — "the moral equivalent

of war" — he called it in an April 1977 address. During his
single term in office, he created the Department of Energy,
established the strategic petroleum reserve, jump-started
the modern solar power industry, advocated conservation
and installed solar panels on the White House roof. In that
1977 speech, Carter used the word "sacrifice" — a word
banished by all presidents since Carter...until President-
elect Barack Obama dragged it out of mothballs and
pressed it into service for his acceptance speech in November 2008.

Rosalynn Carter, for her part, was a partner in the
couple's ethic of Simplicity every step of the way. Her own
symbolic "Thing That Refused to Die" was the gown she
wore to the presidential inaugural ball in 1977; instead of
selecting a new one, she gave a second run to the garment
she'd worn at her husband's gubernatorial gala in 1971.

Our sit-down interview took place at the presidential
suite of the Plains Historic Inn (which both Carters had
helped to decorate and refurbish). The couple was famously
punctual. When Rosalynn Carter took in my silk jacket,
linen skirt and pumps, she apologized for their casual attire.
The former president was wearing an open-collared plaid
shirt, and Rosalynn Carter had on a turquoise corduroy
jacket, slacks and flats.

As an ice-breaker, I quoted from his inaugural address:
"We have learned that more is not necessarily better, that
our great nation has recognized limits." I asked him: "Do
you think Americans would be even more receptive to that
message today?"

"The message is more needed today than it was then,"
the former president responded. "We have become quite
profligate in wasting resources and energy. We don't set an
example for the rest of the world now in the efficiency of
our lives — the simplicity of our lives — that not only saves
energy but enhances the quality of life."

Rosalynn Carter brought her husband's point home, addressing the vicious cycle of material desire and debt that so many people fall victim to: "We think we have to have too much and worry about how we're going to get it and getting it and going into debt for it. Rather than doing without.... I'm sure it would lead to a simpler life if we didn't have to worry about the things we didn't have."

Indeed, after his defeat to Ronald Reagan in 1980, the Carters found solace in their own simple life in Plains, moving back into the 3,200-square-foot brick rancher they'd built in the 1961. They got busy writing books and threw themselves into community life, including joining forces with Habitat for Humanity, which curiously was founded in 1976 in Sumter County (the same rural county that includes Plains) by another dynamic simple-living duo, Millard and Linda Fuller.

Throughout our interview, the former president's keen mind — and positive spirit — was on glistening display. He instantly recalled names of world leaders whom he'd met decades earlier, termed his successor's reversal of his legislation to increase the average miles per gallon in all vehicles made in America from 12 to 28.5 "a real tragedy" and called for America to become a "superpower" — not through military might, but in the promotion of world peace.

The image that stays with me, however, is of the Carters posing for photographs with every group of tourists who show up for his 10 a.m. Sunday School Bible Class at Maranatha Baptist Church. Having witnessed it on two occasions — the second with a video camera rolling — I was struck not only by the generosity of this conscious allocation of their time, but by their briskly efficient process. As soon as they've posed with one group, the next is brought on; conversation is discouraged.

What more fundamental gesture of goodwill could a celebrity offer a fellow human being than immortalizing their moment together? Just as with my travel-mug calculation (if you use throwaway cups every morning for your coffee, after 20 years, you've contributed over 7,000 cups to the landfill), if you aggregate the number of photos the Carters have posed for over the decades, it represents real chunks of time from a couple who are no longer young and are not running for office.

So, how much impact did the *Simple Living with Wanda Urbanska* series have over the course of four seasons with national carriage numbers that fluctuated but reached a high of 75 percent? Of course, it's difficult to say. Our low budgets prohibited such pricey evaluation tools as Nielsen ratings and sophisticated focus groups; almost all of our feedback was anecdotal and overwhelmingly positive. Our series provided modeling for some, light-bulb moments for others and for many brought dormant lessons about conservation and frugality — buried by the cultural·tidal wave of consumerism — to the fore. I'll never forget one viewer's comment, after seeing my on-camera case for carrying a travel mug: "What I got from your show is that if I don't have my travel mug when I'm out, I don't *deserve* coffee."

So what have *I* learned from my near-decade of Simplicity-advocacy on TV? I draw inspiration from many heroes I have had the good fortune to meet, interview and sometimes befriend. I think of Carol Holst, Ed Begley Jr., Bill McKibben, Stan King, Pilar Gerasimo, Michelle Singletary, among others, and am drawn to their earnest conviction to walk the talk, to live by high standards. I remind myself to pick up that trash-bound paperclip, to turn off the drip on a shower in the gym (even if I didn't cause it), to offer a smile and pleasantry to those I encounter.

In hearing people's stories, I see that change is a permanent part of every narrative, every landscape. Just as the medium of television shows early signs of giving way to the powerful forces of the fast-approaching Internet, the time to pare down, to call an end to our national party of wastefulness and excess, to set a better example for the world and ourselves, is upon us.

It has been gratifying to me and my colleagues to see more and more people come to their senses and climb on board, eager to find ways to stop living large and start living small and slow and green. Most recently, in 2008 — the year of the Great Recession — many more have had no choice but to hunker down and simplify. But we survived. We drove less, walked more and in many cases doubled up at home. The holidays came and went with fewer presents. Hey, isn't that what Simplicity advocates have been trying to sell for years?

And, you know, that viewer was right. Simple living *is* about bringing consciousness into our lives and overcoming entitlement. If you're out and you've forgotten your travel mug, you don't *deserve* coffee. And, if you make this small sacrifice this time, you're almost certain to remember to bring it the next.

Voluntary Simplicity: Cool Lifestyle for a Hot Planet

by Duane Elgin

DUANE ELGIN, the author of *Voluntary Simplicity, The Living Universe, Promise Ahead, and Awakening Earth*, is an internationally recognized visionary, speaker and author. He has worked as a senior social scientist at SRI International and with a Presidential Commission on the American Future. He has an MBA from the Wharton Business School and an MA in economic history from the University of Pennsylvania. Duane has co-founded three non-profit organizations working for media accountability and an empowered democracy. In 2006, he received the international Goi Peace Award in recognition of his contribution to a global "vision, consciousness and lifestyle" that fosters a "more sustainable and spiritual culture." His website is awakeningearth.org.

TIME IS UP! The wake-up alarm is buzzing with news ranging from climate disruption to the end of cheap energy and food riots around the world. The time for changes in how we live is *now*. Only if we act swiftly and voluntarily, can we transform catastrophe into opportunity. Small steps are not sufficient. We require large-scale changes in our energy systems, the radical redesign of our urban environments, a conscious democracy with the strength to make great changes, and much more. As individuals, we may protest that we are helpless in the face of such immense challenges and that there is little we can do. However, the reality is just the opposite — only changes in our individual lives can provide a trustworthy foundation for a human future where we can not only maintain ourselves, but also surpass ourselves.

Voluntary Simplicity is a cool lifestyle for a hot planet. Simplicity that is consciously chosen, deliberate and intentional supports a higher quality of life. Here are some of the important reasons to consciously choose Simplicity:

- Simplicity fosters a more harmonious relationship with the Earth — the land, air and water.
- Simplicity promotes fairness and equity among the people of the Earth.
- Simplicity cuts through needless clutter and complexity.
- Simplicity enhances living with balance — inner and outer, work and family, family and community.
- Simplicity reveals the beauty and intelligence of nature's designs.
- Simplicity increases the resources available for future generations.
- Simplicity helps save animal and plant species from extinction.
- Simplicity responds to global shortages of oil, water and other vital resources.
- Simplicity keeps our eyes on the prize of what matters most in our lives — the quality of our relationships with family, friends, community, nature and cosmos.
- Simplicity yields lasting satisfactions that more than compensate for the fleeting pleasures of consumerism.

- Simplicity fosters the sanity of self-discovery and an integrated approach to life.
- Simplicity blossoms in community and connects us to the world with a sense of belonging and common purpose.
- Simplicity is a lighter lifestyle that fits elegantly into the real world of the 21st century.

Voluntary Simplicity is not sacrifice.
- Sacrifice is a consumer lifestyle that is overstressed, overbusy and overworked.
- Sacrifice is investing long hours doing work that is neither meaningful nor satisfying.
- Sacrifice is being apart from family and community to earn a living.
- Sacrifice is the stress of commuting long distances and coping with traffic.
- Sacrifice is the white noise of civilization blotting out the subtle sounds of nature.
- Sacrifice is hiding nature's beauty behind a jumble of billboard advertisements.
- Sacrifice is the smell of the city stronger than the scent of the Earth.
- Sacrifice is carrying more than 200 toxic chemicals in our bodies with consequences that will cascade for generations ahead.
- Sacrifice is the massive extinction of plants and animals and a dramatically impoverished biosphere. Sacrifice is being cut off from nature's wildness and wisdom.
- Sacrifice is global climate disruption, crop failure, famine and forced migration.
- Sacrifice is the absence of feelings of neighborliness and community.
- Sacrifice is feeling divided among the different parts of

our lives and unsure how they work together in a coherent whole.

- Sacrifice is the lost opportunity for soulful encounter with others.

Consumerism offers lives of sacrifice where Simplicity offers lives of opportunity. Simplicity creates the opportunity for greater fulfillment in work, compassion for others, feelings of kinship with all life and awe of living in a living universe. I find it ironic that a life-way of Simplicity that can take us into an opportunity-filled future is often portrayed in the mass media as primitive or regressive and pulling back from opportunity. Specifically, here are three major ways that I see the idea of "simplicity" presented in today's popular media:

Crude/Regressive Simplicity

The mainstream media often present Simplicity as a path of regress instead of progress. Simplicity is frequently viewed as anti-technology, anti-innovation and a backward-looking way of life that seeks a romantic return to a bygone era. A regressive Simplicity is often portrayed as a utopian, back-to-nature movement with families leaving the stresses of an urban life in favor of living on a farm or in a recreational vehicle or on a boat. This is a stereotypical view of a crudely simple lifestyle — a throwback to an earlier time and more primitive condition — with no indoor toilet, no phone, no computer, no television and no car. No thanks! Seen in this way, Simplicity is a cartoon lifestyle that seems naive, disconnected and irrelevant — an approach to living that can be easily dismissed as impractical and unworkable. Regarding Simplicity as regressive and primitive makes it easier to embrace a business-as-usual approach to living in the world.

Cosmetic/Superficial Simplicity

In recent years, a different view of Simplicity has begun to appear — a cosmetic Simplicity that attempts to cover over deep defects in our modern ways of living by giving the appearance of meaningful change. Shallow Simplicity assumes that green technologies — such as fuel-efficient cars, fluorescent light bulbs and recycling — will fix our problems, give us breathing room and allow us to continue pretty much as we have in the past without requiring that we make fundamental changes in how we live and work. Cosmetic Simplicity puts green lipstick on our unsustainable lives to give them the outward appearance of health and happiness. A superficial Simplicity gives a false sense of security by implying that small measures will solve great challenges. A cosmetic Simplicity perpetuates the status quo by assuming that, with the use of green technologies, we can moderate our impact and continue along our current path of growth for another half century or more.

Sophisticated/Conscious Simplicity

Seldom presented in the mass media and poorly understood is an elegant Simplicity that represents a deep, graceful and sophisticated transformation in our ways of living — the work that we do, the transportation that we use, the homes and neighborhoods in which we live, the food that we eat, the clothes that we wear and much more. A sophisticated and graceful Simplicity seeks to heal our relationship with the Earth, with one another and with the sacred universe. Conscious Simplicity is not simple. This is a life-way that is growing and flowering with a garden of expressions. Sophisticated Simplicity fits aesthetically and sustainably into the real world of the 21st century.

Which of these expressions of Simplicity — crude, cosmetic or sophisticated — is most fitting in our dramatically changing world?

Which Kind of Simplicity Fits Our World?

Global trends indicate that a perfect "world storm" is developing rapidly — a planetary-scale systems crisis — that will push the human family to make deep and lasting changes in our approach to living. We now confront the simultaneous challenges of the growing disruption of the global climate, an enormous increase in human populations living in gigantic cities, the depletion of vital resources such as fresh water and cheap oil, the massive and rapid extinction of animal and plant species around the world, growing disparities between the rich and the poor made starkly visible with the communications revolution and the spread of weapons of mass destruction. We are being pushed to wake up and learn to live far more sustainably by making profound changes in our manner of living, consuming, working and relating.

Simplicity is not an alternative lifestyle for a marginal few; it is a creative choice for the mainstream majority, particularly in developed nations. If we are to pull together as a human community, I believe that it will be crucial that people in affluent nations embrace the choice of a deep and sophisticated Simplicity as a foundation for sustainability. *Simplicity is simultaneously a personal choice, a civilizational choice and a species choice.* Even with major technological innovations in energy and transportation, it will require dramatic changes in our overall levels and patterns of living and consuming if we are to maintain the integrity of the Earth as a living system. Overall, a "deep Simplicity" that fosters an elegant transformation of our lives is vital if we are to build a workable and meaningful future.

What does a life of Voluntary Simplicity or Earth-friendly living look like? There is no cookbook we can turn to with easy recipes for the simple life in the modern era. The world is moving into new territory, and we are inventing green living as we evolve. For more than 30 years, I've explored the simple life, and I've found such a diversity of expressions that the most useful and accurate way of describing this approach to living is with the metaphor of a garden.

A Garden of Simplicity

To portray the richness of Simplicity, here are seven different flowerings of expression that I see growing in the "garden of simplicity." Although overlapping, each expression of Simplicity seems sufficiently distinct to warrant a separate category.

Uncluttered Simplicity

Simplicity means taking charge of lives that are too busy, too stressed, and too fragmented. Simplicity means cutting back on clutter, complexity and trivial distractions, both material and non-material, and focusing on the essentials — whatever those may be for each of our unique lives. As Thoreau said, "Our life is frittered away by detail. Simplify, simplify." Or, as Plato wrote, "In order to seek one's own direction, one must simplify the mechanics of ordinary, everyday life."

Ecological Simplicity

Simplicity means to choose ways of living that touch the Earth more lightly and that reduce our ecological impact on the web of life. This life-path remembers our deep roots with the Earth, air and water. It encourages us to connect with nature, the seasons and the cosmos. A natural Simplicity feels a deep reverence for the community of life on Earth and accepts that the non-human realms of plants and animals have their dignity and rights as well the human.

Compassionate Simplicity

Simplicity means to feel such a strong sense of kinship with others that we "choose to live simply so that others may simply live." A compassionate Simplicity means feeling a bond with the community of life and being drawn toward a path of reconciliation — with other species and future generations as well as, for example, between those with great differences of wealth and opportunity. A compassionate Simplicity is a path of cooperation and fairness that seeks a future of mutually assured development for all.

Soulful Simplicity

Simplicity means to approach life as a meditation and to cultivate our experience of intimate connection with all that exists. By living simply, we can more directly awaken to the living universe that surrounds and sustains us, moment by moment. Soulful Simplicity is more concerned with consciously tasting life in its unadorned richness than with a particular standard or manner of material living. In cultivating a soulful connection with life, we tend to look beyond surface appearances and bring our interior aliveness into relationships of all kinds.

Business Simplicity

Simplicity means a new kind of economy is growing in the world with many expressions of "right livelihood" in the rapidly growing market for healthy and sustainable products and services of all kinds — from home building materials and energy systems to foods and transportation. When the need for a sustainable infrastructure in developing nations is combined with the need to retrofit and redesign the homes, cities, workplaces and transportation systems of developed nations, it is clear that an enormous wave of green economic activity will unfold. A new economics is integral to this new approach to business, for example, where "waste equals food" or the waste of one activity represents resources for another part of the production system.

Civic Simplicity

Simplicity means a new approach to governing ourselves, recognizing that to live more lightly and sustainably on the Earth will require changes in every area of public life — from transportation and education to the design of our cities, public buildings and workplaces. The politics of Simplicity is also a media politics as the mass media are the primary vehicle for reinforcing, or transforming, the mass consciousness of consumerism.

Frugal Simplicity

Simplicity means that, by cutting back on spending that is not truly serving our lives and by practicing skillful management of our personal finances, we can achieve greater financial independence. Frugality and careful financial management bring increased financial freedom and the opportunity to more consciously choose our path through life. Living with less also decreases the impact of our consumption upon the Earth and frees resources for others.

As these seven approaches illustrate, the growing culture of Simplicity contains a flourishing garden of expressions whose great diversity — and intertwined unity — are creating a resilient and hardy ecology of learning about how to live more sustainable and meaningful lives. As with other ecosystems, it is the diversity of expressions that fosters flexibility, adaptability and resilience. Because there are so many pathways of great relevance into the garden of Simplicity, this cultural movement appears to have enormous potential to grow.

[Note: This chapter was adapted from the third edition of Duane's book *Voluntary Simplicity*, New York, HarperCollins, 2009.]

Graceful Living

by Jerome Segal

JEROME SEGAL has had a diverse career as a philosopher, political activist, Congressional aide and policy analyst. He obtained a PhD in philosophy from the University of Michigan, taught at the University of Pennsylvania and obtained an MPA from the Hubert Humphrey School of Public Affairs before moving to Washington DC to work for Congressman Donald Fraser. During the Carter administration, he became Coordinator for the Near East in the policy bureau of the US Agency for International Development and, later, Senior Advisor for Agency Planning. After leaving government, he joined the Institute for Philosophy and Public Policy at the University of Maryland where he is presently a Senior Research Scholar. In 1989 he founded The Jewish Peace Lobby and remains its president. Jerome is the author of five books, *Agency and Alienation: A Theory of Human Presence, Creating the Palestinian State: A Strategy for Peace; Negotiating Jerusalem, Graceful Simplicity: The Philosophy and Politics of the Alternative American Dream* and, most recently, *Joseph's Bones: Understanding the Struggle Between God and Mankind in the Bible.*

FOR THOSE OF US in the broad middle class, it is often hard to say what is wrong with the way we live. It is not some single element, nor is it anything that we could plug in here and there and have things be radically different. It is a quality that pervades life in its entirety; my word for it is "gracefulness." Within our contemporary world, what is most striking is the near total absence of gracefulness. I focus on it not because it represents all that is important, but because it seems to me that which is most absent, even from the lives of those thought to be successful.

Understood as a quality of life, gracefulness is not what we readily associate with simple living. When we think of graceful living, the most natural way of picturing such a life is to see it as free of care and to see that freedom as emerging from abundance, indeed, from overabundance, an abundance that is suffused with security and ease. The vision is not merely one of wealth but of the enjoyment of wealth, indeed, of the effortless enjoyment of wealth. It is not just money; it is money possessed and used with style — being elegantly wealthy, not just having tasteful things, but consuming them tastefully. In short, graceful living seems to imply a mastery of the art of being wealthy.

We typically associate such style not just with money, but with old money — that is, with money that one is comfortable with to the point of second nature. It is money that not only serves life through the things of beauty that it provides, but does so effortlessly. Moreover, it is money that is attained gracefully. The magazines that picture graceful consumption rarely mention what one does to make that consumption possible. Indeed, it might break the spell if we knew. The implicit assumption, if not of inherited wealth, is that money comes easily.

It is not hard to disparage such images, but there is something terribly important to be learned about how to move gracefully in the world of things. This is not easily done; the ability to live gracefully, even for those who are rich, may require more than one generation. It may be that attaining this art of graceful living is something that is achieved over many years and is handed down through the family — a tradition of knowing how to live and be.

Later I will argue that graceful existence does not depend upon significant material wealth, and indeed, to pursue gracefulness through material acquisition is a fool's quest. For now, however, my aim is to explore gracefulness itself. Just what is it? Whether or not an abundance of possessions is required, a graceful life is one of beauty, security, comfort, ease and naturalness. It is a life that is free from overriding anxiety and ceaseless striving. It is largely peaceful rather than hectic. There may be adventure and challenge, but it is a life that does not suffer from constant hassle and hustle. As such, gracefulness is an achievement within the aesthetic of being. For most of us, except for rare islands in time, modern life is utterly devoid of gracefulness.

To live gracefully is to live within flowing rhythms at a human pace. It need not always be the same. There is gracefulness in fast dances and in slow dances — but most of us are not dancing at all. In a graceful life, there is time to pay respect to the value of what you do, to the worth of those you care for and to the possessions you own. Gracefulness is not possible when life is frenetic, when we are harried or suffer from overload, time crunch and a vast multiplicity of commitments and pressures.

When I first considered the term "graceful," in addition to its association with opulence, I had reservations because of its religious connotations. Saying grace and receiving grace initially seemed to be notions that have little to do with what is under discussion. In that I was wrong. Important linkages exist between grace in the religious sense and gracefulness as an aesthetic of life. Whether religion has any place in one's life or not, there are connections that are worth pondering. Consider the act of saying grace before a meal. Here the core is an attitude of thanksgiving, of appreciation. The focus is on recognizing the full value of what one has, rather than lamenting what one does not. While one can mouth the words, one cannot authentically begin a meal with a benediction of grace and at the same time maintain a sense of dissatisfaction with what one has. There is a certain peaceful contentment that is part of genuine thankfulness.

When one does approach a meal gracefully, one can look in two different directions. One can consider what one has against the "perspective of less," contrasting what one has with what others do not. This means seeing things against the backdrop of poverty, of hunger, of times and places of suffering and deprivation. Here the act of consumption is also a moment to see oneself and one's situation within the broader perspective of human experience and, so seen, to be thankful for what one has and more aware of what one has been lucky enough not to have experienced. Thus, one is thankful to have something to eat when others have starved. And one is thankful to have friends and loved ones to share the meal with when others are lonely, and when there may come a day when those friends and loved ones are gone.

Then there is another perspective, one that does not take its power from the contrast with deprivation and suffering, but rather seeks to put us in touch with the abundance in front of us. Here the appreciation of the food rests not on an awareness of hunger, but on how good this food is, of how remarkable a thing is the simple potato or the diverse ingredients of a salad or the crust on a good bread. And then to look around the table and take stock of those who are there, valuing them not against the possibility of loneliness but in virtue of the richness that they provide.

Here appreciativeness goes beyond thankfulness, to being open to the values that are inherent in something. This kind of appreciativeness requires a certain kind of experiencing. It is not primarily a matter of intellectual assent, but of an openness, of an accessibility to what is valuable, be it another person, a piece of music, a work of art, a spring day or a great ball game. Often such appreciation is most present when we are young, when the world is fresh. As we age and as we get into our harnesses, our ability to take pleasure dulls. In other contexts, appreciation is not automatically present but is the result of learning and exposure: for example, the appreciation of art and music, especially if it comes from other cultures.

This appreciativeness is an orientation that we bring (or more likely, fail to bring) to any of the things of ordinary life. Thus, with respect to food and meals, we may be oblivious to the difference between good cooking and bad, oblivious to the pleasure of eating off a handsome dining table versus a card table. We may be blind to the value of those we eat with, blind to those we live with, blind to those we parent.

Yet for this second kind of appreciation to be valid, there has to be something there to be appreciated. What if the tomatoes taste like rubber, the food is overcooked, the bread is dismal, the spouse is in a foul mood and the children are obnoxious? Where is gracefulness then? What is there that is worthy of appreciation?

Thus, in this second sense, a graceful meal requires more than the appropriate attitude; it also involves the presence of a qualitative richness, what we might call "good fortune," so long as we do not view ourselves as passive with respect to whether such fortune is before us. This links to another dimension of the act of saying grace. The grace ritual requires that we take a moment before digging in, a moment of pause, a moment of quiet that gives a certain dignity to the meal. It separates it from what precedes it. In spirit, if not in practice, the initial benediction establishes a space that pervades the entire meal. When we have a meal in this way, we do not wolf down our food. We set the meal apart; the benediction allows us to break with the hectic pace of a busy day. To an extent, it turns the meal into a ceremony. As such, it is not only a space worthy of appreciation; it is a space worthy of taking the time and energy to create properly.

Saying grace is not necessary for graceful living, nor as I understand it, does saying grace require any religious belief. But in its authentic form, making the dinner table a place of grace can be an important constitutive element of the aesthetic of a life of Simplicity.

Another connotation of grace is found within some religious traditions (the idea of receiving something "by the grace of God") that may also seem at first only a different notion of grace, one that has nothing to do with the kind of graceful living under discussion. Here we are dealing with a theological doctrine that during the 16th and 17th centuries was the subject of fierce debate within Christianity. At issue was the question of how one attained salvation. Was salvation attained "through works," that is, through living righteously in accord with religious commandments, through doing good, through attaining merit, through living a life that deserved to be saved? Or was salvation something that could not be obtained through the fulfillment of a contract? Was it the case that nothing that we could do could compel, even morally compel, God to dispense salvation? If we were to be saved it was through the free gift, through the grace of God alone.

What, if any, relationship does this religious conception of grace have to graceful living? Some of those within such religious traditions might maintain that it is only through the grace of God that we can ourselves attain a truly grace-ful existence. But this is not what I have in mind. Rather, it seems to me that in the religious conception it is God who is graceful. He is the dispenser, and what he gives he gives out of his grace; that is to say, he gives out of his bounty, not because he has to, not because he is morally compelled to and not because we have earned it or covenanted for it.

Social existence is primarily a matter of giving to others and receiving from them. To live gracefully in a world of others implies gracefulness in these interactions. Yet this is what is sorely missing in our lives. On the most fundamen-tal level, we are too busy and too self-engaged to give much time or attention to others. What we do give is often limited to what we sense we are obligated to provide. Often what is done is done reluctantly, resentfully or stingily. This stingi-ness runs through our relationships, be they fixed patterns of exchange or diverse social relations, be they relations be-tween husband and wife, between parent and child, between friends, between boss and worker, between colleagues or between telephone operator and caller. We don't have the time, patience or interest for the other often enough, even for those we call friends.

The flip side of this, however, is that people need oppor-tunities to give of themselves. Often enough we long to be of importance to someone else. When there is no receptive-ness to what we might want to give, we are bottled up, pre-vented from coming more fully into existence — whether by others, by the structures of interaction or by structures of production. Thus, we may find ourselves devoid of signif-icant opportunity, or devoid of the skills or simply devoid of much to give. This inability to give is a great tragedy, and its roots may be educational and social as much as psychologi-cal. The great educational project is for each of us to develop so that we have something significant to give to others, and the great social project is to have structures of human exchange, both in the economic realm and outside it, that provide the opportunity to give what riches we have.

Thus, as we think of Simplicity, seeing it through the lens of graceful living brings deeper understanding.

[Note: This chapter was adapted from *Graceful Simplicity: Towards a Philosophy and Politics of Simple Living*, New York, Henry Holt and Company, 1999.]

A Scientific Approach to Voluntary Simplicity

by Tim Kasser and
Kirk Warren Brown

TIM KASSER, PhD, is a professor of psychology at Knox College in Galesburg, Illinois. He is the author of *The High Price of Materialism*, co-editor of *Psychology and Consumer Culture* and the author of over 60 scientific articles and book chapters on values, well-being, consumerism and other topics. Professionally, the issue of Voluntary Simplicity attracts him, given its strong congruence with the empirical distinction his research has made between "intrinsic" values focused on personal growth, close relationships and working to benefit the broader community versus "extrinsic" values focused on money, image and status. Personally, the topic of Voluntary Simplicity holds lasting appeal, given that he lives with his wife, two son, and assorted animals on 10 acres in the Western Illinois countryside.

KIRK WARREN BROWN, PhD, is an assistant professor of psychology at Virginia Commonwealth University. His research centers on the role of attention to and awareness of internal states and behavior in self-regulation and well-being. He has written numerous scholarly publications on the role of mindfulness and mindfulness training in enhancing emotion regulation, behavior regulation, mental health and lifestyle choices. His research is funded by several federal granting agencies and non-profit foundations.

AUTHORS WRITING about Voluntary Simplicity (VS) have long suggested that this lifestyle can foster both personal happiness and ecological sustainability. As scientists, however, we have been struck by the fact that remarkably little carefully controlled research has been conducted to investigate the purported personal and societal benefits of VS. To address this gap, we set out to test whether the VS lifestyle helps to promote both a life of personal fulfillment and a more sustainable culture.[1] In this chapter, we describe our research study and its findings.

The Research Study

We sought to broadly represent the experiences and lifestyle choices of simplifiers in America and, therefore, recruited 200 adults who considered themselves to be living lives of Voluntary Simplicity. They came from 42 states and the District of Columbia and were an average of 43 years old; two-thirds of them were women. For comparison purposes, we also recruited a group of 200 mainstream Americans who were matched to the VS group by geographic region, sex, age and race/ethnicity. We undertook this careful matching procedure to reduce the possibility that any differences we found between VS and mainstream Americans in happiness and ecological behavior were simply due to basic demographic factors or to basic geographic differences like living in an urban or rural setting.

While we relied primarily upon our respondents to tell us whether they were living simply or not, we also supported this self-reported distinction between the VS and mainstream groups by asking all participants whether they had voluntarily chosen to earn less than they could earn and had voluntarily chosen to spend less than they could spend; these are standard criteria for VS often noted in the popular literature.[2] The VS group was significantly more likely than the mainstream group to have voluntarily made both of these choices in the last five years,[3] suggesting that the participants' self-identification as Voluntary Simplifiers was a valid way of categorizing the groups.

The 400 Americans in our groups completed a detailed survey that included questions about their happiness and their environmentally relevant behavior. To measure happiness, participants answered questions from two widely used, well-validated measures tapping the three main components of what is technically termed "subjective well-being": life satisfaction (e.g., "My current life is ideal for me."), frequency of pleasant emotions (e.g., happy, joyful) and (in)frequency of unpleasant emotions (e.g., frustrated, worried/anxious).[4] We used two other measures to assess participants' ecological behavior.[5] First, we asked how often they engaged in 54 different positive environmental behaviors, ranging from recycling to reusing old items to political involvement in ecological causes. Second, the study participants completed the Ecological Footprint Questionnaire, which gathers information about diet (e.g., meat-eating versus vegetarian), home-related energy consumption and transportation choices (e.g., miles of car and airplane travel per year). A complex algorithm was then applied to participants' answers in order to compute the number of hectares (1 hectare = 2.47 acres) required to maintain their lifestyle choices — their ecological footprint. A smaller footprint reflects a lower-impact lifestyle.

Scientists are keenly interested in "parsimony," or having the simplest possible explanation for something that is also most consistent with what is already known. Because

VS is the "new kid on the block," scientifically speaking it must therefore contend with other factors that studies have already shown are associated with happiness and sustainability. VS has to show that it can explain something that established factors do not. In our study, besides measuring whether someone was pursuing a simplifier or mainstream lifestyle, we also measured two variables that past research found were associated with happiness and sustainability: mindfulness and values.

Mindfulness refers to a receptive state of mind in which attention is brought to bear on what is occurring in the present. When people are mindful, they are more likely to "see" internal and external realities clearly, openly and without distortion. A growing body of research on mindfulness shows that people vary considerably in the level of mindful attention they give to their thoughts, emotions and behaviors, and that to the extent they are more mindful, they report a higher sense of well-being. Some psychologists have also conjectured that mindfulness promotes more sustainable behavior, as it encourages reflection on the ecological impact of one's behavior and may lessen one's susceptibility to the onslaught of consumerist messages that encourage materialistic — and ultimately, environmentally damaging — pursuits.[6]

Values concern what people believe is important in life, and substantial research across a variety of cultures and age groups supports a fundamental distinction between two types of values: materialistic and intrinsic.[7] Materialistic values are widely encouraged in contemporary consumer society and concern the acquisition of money, possessions, image and status. In contrast, intrinsic values are focused on self-acceptance and personal growth, close relationships with family and friends and contribution to the community and the larger world and are theorized to offer more direct satisfaction and fulfillment. Indeed, a substantial body of research shows that when people orient their lives around intrinsic values, they report higher levels of well-being and lower levels of distress than when they are oriented toward materialistic values. Additionally, a growing body of research shows that materialistic values promote ecologically destructive attitudes and behaviors, whereas intrinsic values promote more sustainable ecological attitudes and behaviors.[8]

The Study Findings

Recall that the overall purpose of the project was to determine whether or not it is possible to live a life that is both happy and sustainable, and to see whether or not identifying oneself as a Voluntary Simplifier helps explain the presumed compatibility of happiness and sustainability, even after accounting for more established factors like mindfulness and values.

Our statistical analyses showed that happiness and sustainability were indeed compatible. That is, people who reported being more satisfied with their lives and experiencing more pleasant than unpleasant emotions were also more likely to report doing more ecologically sustainable behaviors and having lower ecological footprints.

While there was some evidence that Voluntary Simplifiers were happier than mainstream Americans and were living more sustainable lives, ultimately our statistical analyses[9] showed that identifying as a Voluntary Simplifier (versus a mainstream American) was not as important as being mindful and being oriented toward intrinsic values (relative to materialistic values). The same was also true if we used the distinction between people who reported making a voluntary reduction in their income and spending versus people who had not; it was still the case that happy, sustainable lives were best explained by being mindful and pursuing intrinsic rather than materialistic values.

Implications of the Research

A primary take-home message of the findings of this study is that living more happily and more lightly on the Earth is not as much about whether people think of themselves as Voluntary Simplifiers, but instead is more about their inner life — that is, whether they are living in a conscious, mindful way and with a set of values organized around intrinsic fulfillment. Ultimately, we believe, this is basically what authors writing about Simplicity have proposed for many years. For example, as Duane Elgin has noted, VS is an attempt "to encounter life more consciously"[10] or with greater attunement to the richness of life in the present moment.[11] In addition, VS is almost always described as a lifestyle that entails letting go of the materialistic values of the dominant consumer culture to instead focus on the "inner riches" — that is, the intrinsic values of personal development, relationships and community.

In sum, then, if readers of this book seek to promote happy, sustainable lifestyles, our study findings suggest that, rather than focusing on VS per se, a more productive approach may be to cultivate a way of life that encourages mindfulness and intrinsic values. Indeed, our experience talking with many mainstream Americans suggests that many people find the idea of "simplifying" their lives to be a confusing and difficult concept. Perhaps people would respond more positively to the idea of living in a more mindful, less harried way and of shifting their lifestyles away from values focused on materialism and instead toward aspirations that nurture personal development, affiliation and community contribution.[12]

Finding Real Wealth: Twice the Value for Half the Resources

by Dave Wann

DAVID WANN wrote *Simple Prosperity: Finding Real Wealth in a Sustainable Lifestyle*, a sequel to the best-selling book he co-authored, *Affluenza: The All-Consuming Epidemic*, which is now in nine languages. He is the producer of the award-winning TV documentary *Designing a Great Neighborhood* as well as the short program *Building Livable Communities*.

TAKEN AS A WHOLE, we North Americans are overfed but undernourished. Socially, psychologically and physically, we are not fully meeting human needs. Although the TV commercials would have us believe that every itch can be scratched with a trip to the mall, the truth is we're consuming more now but enjoying it less. According to surveys taken by the US National Science Foundation for the past 30 years, even with steady increases in income, our level of overall happiness has actually tapered off.

Why? Many believe it's because a lifestyle of overconsumption creates deficiencies in things that we really need, like health, social connections, security and discretionary time. These deficiencies leave us vulnerable to daily lives of dependency, passive consumption — working, watching and waiting. The typical urban resident waits in line five years of his or her life and spends six months sitting at red lights, eight months opening junk mail, one year searching for misplaced items and four years cleaning house. Every year, the typical high-school student spends 1,500 hours in front of the tube, compared with 900 hours spent at school. And this in not just an American addiction: a 2004 French survey representing 2.5 *billion people* in 72 countries documented an average of 3.5 hours of TV watched every day!

Yet, the game is changing. Just as we approach an all-time peak in consumption, converging variables like shrinking resource supplies, necessitate changes in the way we live. Here's the good news: reducing our levels of consumption will not be a sacrifice but a bonus if we simply redefine the meaning of the word "success."

Instead of more stuff in our already-stuffed lives, we can choose fewer things but better things of higher quality, fewer visits to the doctor and more visits to museums and the houses of friends. Greater use of our hands and minds in creative activities like playing a flute or building a new kitchen table. If we are successful as a culture, we'll get more value from each transaction, each relationship and each unit of energy; by reducing the waste and carelessness that now litter our economy — energy hogs like aluminum cans and plastic bottles, huge thirsty lawns, excessive airplane travel, feedlot meat and suburbs without stores — we can finance the coming transition to a lifestyle that feels more comfortable in the present and doesn't clearcut the future.

Value Shift

Imagine a way of life that's culturally richer but materially leaner. In this emerging lifestyle, there is less stress, insecurity, pollution, doubt and debt but more vacation time, more solid connections with nature and more participation in the arts, amateur sports and politics. Greater reliance on human energy — fueled by complex carbohydrates — and less reliance on ancient sunlight stored as pollution-filled fossil fuel. Fewer fluorescent hours in the supermarket, more sunny afternoons out in the vegetable garden. Instead of being passive consumers, doggedly treadmilling to keep up with overproduction, we'll choose healthy, renewable forms of wealth such as social capital (networks and bonds of trust), whose value increases the more we spend it, stimulating work that's more like a puzzle than a prison sentence, and acquired skills and interests that enhance our free time, making money less of a stressful imperative.

A culture shift like this — from an emphasis on material wealth to an abundance of time, relationships and experiences — has already occurred in many societies such as 18th-century Japan. Land was in short supply, forest resources were being depleted, and minerals such as gold and copper were suddenly scarce as well. Japan's culture adapted by developing a national ethic that centered on moderation and efficiency. An attachment to the material things in life was seen as demeaning, while the advancement of crafts and human knowledge were lofty goals. Quality became ingrained in a culture that eventually produced world-class solar cells and Toyota Priuses. Training and education in aesthetics and ritualistic arts flourished, resulting in disciplines like fencing, martial arts, the tea ceremony, flower arranging, literature, art and mastery of the abacus. The three largest cities in Japan had 1,500 bookstores among them, and most people had access to basic education, health care and the necessities of life, further enriching a culture that spent less money but paid more attention.

Places such as Canada and the European Union (EU) have already started down this enviable path, making political and cultural space for values that lie *beneath* the bottom line of monetary wealth. For example, most EU countries give legal standing to mandatory family leave from work, part-time jobs with pro-rated benefits, higher taxes on energy use and pollution in exchange for lower income taxes and take-back laws requiring manufacturers to recycle products at the end of their use. An everyday ethic is emerging in Europe that encourages sustainable behavior by popular demand. Says John de Graaf, co-author of *Affluenza: The All-Consuming Epidemic*, "Western European countries have invested in their social contracts. Strategic investments in health care, education, transportation, and public space reduced the need (and desire) of individuals to maximize their own incomes."

On the other hand, in places such as the US and Australia, subsidized development patterns and an ingrained quest for privacy and consumption often spin off unhealthy isolation. A 2007 National Science Foundation study in the US reported that one-fourth of all Americans have *no one* they can confide in or celebrate with, and the inner circles of the rest have fallen from about three confidants to two. Our need to elevate social connections to a higher priority is literally a matter of life and death. In one study reported by Dr. Dean Ornish in *Love and Survival*, men and women who were about to have open-heart surgery were asked two questions: Do you draw strength from your religious faith? and Are you a member of a group of people who get together on a regular basis? Those who said no to both questions were dead within six months, compared to only three percent of those who said yes to both.

Another primordial human need is connection with nature. When people view slides of meadows and streams, their blood pressure falls; and hospital patients with a view of trees go home sooner than those whose view is a brick wall. When people with Attention Deficit Hyperactivity Disorder spend time in nature, the results are often as effective as Ritalin. Yet Americans are increasingly creatures of the great indoors, and sterilized, manicured landscapes. For example, some geometric school playgrounds now display signs that say, "No running!" The design of playgrounds often excludes the rough, green edges of nature where kids love to play; instead the aim is to minimize liability, reduce maintenance and improve surveillance.

Healthy, robust cultures mentor diets that are anthropologically correct, but sadly, in many market-bound economies, food has fallen from its lofty stature as a source of well-being, community and clarity to the simplistic category of fun. "Even wild monkeys have healthier diets than many humans," says anthropologist Katharine Milton. Again, in our money-mad world, the focus is on snackability, convenience and shelf life rather than *human life*. Alarmingly, the value of the food has radically declined in the last century. In 1900, wheat from conventional farms was 90 percent protein, compared to only 9 percent today, according to United Nations data. Popeye would have to eat a hundred or more cans of supermarket spinach to get the energy-boosting iron he got from one can back in the 1950s, when soil was still rich in minerals and enzymes.

How can we reclaim our vanishing psychological, physical and spiritual nutrients? How can we make political and cultural space for these most critical needs? To give a few examples, one school dramatically reduced vandalism and violence by simply taking out the pop machines and replacing cafeteria fast foods like pizza and burgers with salad bars, fruits and fresh vegetables. New ways of building and rebuilding neighborhoods are helping residents create social networks of trust and support, at the same time preserving habitat and providing great places to exercise. Cities are stepping forward to ban trans fats, set global warming targets, tax bottled water and train organic farmers. We're beginning to steer the economy in a different *direction* that minimizes unnecessary consumption but optimizes contentment. Rather than remaining trapped in an economic box of outdated assumptions, we are speaking out in favor of a joyfully moderate, compassionate economy that delivers a higher proportion of health, hope and happiness.

[David Wann has written nine books. For more information about his work and writing, see davewann.com.]

Religion
and the Earth

by Rev. Canon Sally Bingham

SALLY BINGHAM has brought widespread attention to
the link between religious faith and the environment
through her work on The Regeneration Project and the
Interfaith Power and Light campaign. As one of the first
faith leaders to fully recognize global warming as a core
moral issue, she has mobilized thousands of religious
people to put their faith into action through energy
stewardship. Sally serves as the Environmental Minister at Grace Cathedral in San Francisco, and chairs the
Commission on the Environment for the Diocese of
California where she was installed as Canon for Environmental Ministry.

IT SEEMS THAT religion has been around for over thousands of years. So you would have to agree that religion
is "sustainable." The concept is interesting because one has
to decide if religion sustains itself or whether we the people
sustain it. As we talk about the planet's sustainability, the
same question arises. I think the answers are analogous. The
creator of the world will survive whether people are here or
not, and the same is true of the planet; it will survive without the human race. In both cases, it is human activity that

participates in nurturing (or not) the subject, but the subject itself doesn't need human activity to survive. In many cases, both religion and the planet have suffered *because* of human activity. Rather than honor the true and intended relationships, human activity has had an adverse affect. The diverse doctrines of religion have been massaged to reflect a contemporary society as cultures have developed and changed, and it seems that in the broadest terms religion is here to stay. The belief that something greater than humans is at work in the world persists in the minds of most people. And that divine presence will persist with or without humans to write and argue about it.

Are humans here to stay is a deeper and more relevant question in light of the dysfunctional relationship that humans have with their environment. That "something greater" (for my purposes, God) created a diverse and complicated life system and set it up in order that the species and ecosystems would provide for one another and live in harmony. There would be enough for all if we didn't get overly greedy and selfish. At least that is what I surmise from the Genesis creation story. And one species, the human one, was given "dominion." In this sense, dominion is the responsibility to be sure that everything else is maintained in balance, survives and multiplies. For people of faith, this creation story calls on us to be sustainable, but until recently we didn't know what that meant — we didn't have to know because there was seemingly enough for all, even if we were thoughtless about our waste. There was no thought about future generations and their survival because the vastness and grandeur of our natural resources looked, at least for a time, to be an unending supply of energy and abundance expected to last forever.

It is hard to know just when the notion of sustainability took hold because many people have been aware of an advancing problem for years, but they did not shout it from the rooftops until quite recently. Scientists have known for some time, and certainly the people who read Scripture with a keen eye for preservation of all creation were aware that the destruction of natural resources was a sin. Most religious people understand an intrinsic right to life for all living things. The sustainability notion is relatively new, and I think it has grabbed us now because the consequences of unleashed and irresponsible human activity have begun to take a toll.

This intrinsic right must be respected with one important caveat: Some things have to die so that others might live. This fundamental teaching of Christianity is the view from which this essay is written. In order for the human race to survive, which I believe is God's intention, some plants and animals will die. However, not all animals of one species must die, nor all plants of a particular species. Quite the contrary; remember "be fruitful and multiply"? It is the part of the creation story in which humans were given "dominion" — dominion as in stewardship, not domination or destruction.

According to E. O. Wilson from Harvard, 20,000 species a year are being destroyed. If a sustainable way of life means that the needs of the present are met without compromising future generations' ability to meet their own needs, then this immoral destruction of species is not only sinful, but will contribute to the eventual death of the human species. Humans are at the top of the ladder, having been given a special role to be the caretakers of all else. We cannot sustain ourselves unless we support, nurture and preserve all the species that God created. We are created like an integrated system, a web of life, and each species is connected to another — either dependent upon or visa versa. This interdependent web of life would instruct us, then, to respect each other's place on the ladder of life. Each is important not only to the place it holds on the ladder, but also to God. Destroy one of the places and the whole is affected, leading to the destruction of the species at the top. If the support system is substantially weakened, it remains reasonable then that the top will collapse.

How then are we to survive when so many millions of people are unaware or simply don't understand the problem? I believe that in order to become sustainable our values have to change, and the place that will best encourage a value change is the faith community. This is where we find and instill hope — not without prayer and action, but hope is the glue that will hold people together when they see the potential catastrophic changes going on around the world due to our unprecedented contribution of carbon dioxide and methane to the atmosphere. And they *will* see it. Climate change, the focus of my ministry (the Interfaith Power and Light Campaign), is the most important moral challenge of our time.

Not only is climate change a moral challenge, it is the most destructive situation facing us. It will have to be corrected soon in order not to destroy the healthy lives of future generations. It has been scientifically proven that producing energy from burning fossil fuels is upsetting the balance that God put into place to sustain life. Species extinction, disease, droughts, floods, severe and more frequent storms and more frequent fires all result from too much carbon dioxide in the atmosphere. There was a time when we could afford to be dependent on coal, oil and gas for energy, but like the changes in religion, as cultures change and mature, we have to change and mature our way of producing energy. We cannot solve a problem using the same technology that caused the problem in the first place. There was a time when religion condoned the buying and selling of slaves, but as we matured and became more aware; we realized that owning slaves was immoral. Religion addressed that issue and redefined what it teaches about the dignity of every human being. As the moral voice of religion spoke up against slavery, the will to change that practice began. We need the moral voice of religion again to show that harming creation is a sin. Furthermore we are called to serve the poor who are being disproportionately affected by the changing climate. The poor and vulnerable communities, both here and around the world, contribute the least to the problem but are suffering and will continue to suffer the most. This is unjust and against religious teachings. Serving one another is a religious mandate; exploitation of people is against the will of God.

At the time of this writing, religion is starting to redefine what it means to be human and with that will come a change in values — an awareness that we cannot continue business as usual if we are concerned about future generations. Many religious denominations are putting aside their differences and working together for a sustainable world. As humans discover that our relationship with each other and with the natural world needs to be one of harmony, the necessary changes will come. The same way that religion has evolved with a changing culture, human relationship to the Earth will evolve. The concept that sustainability is a value is establishing itself. Every religious person who declares a love for God and creation must begin to understand that stewardship of creation goes hand and hand with the notion of sustainability. We have the technology, the skills and the resources to take a different road than this potential disastrous one that we are on — a road toward the end of life. We must strive for the will to change our values, and for our political leaders to work on behalf of human survival and focus on a bigger picture than the next election.

God created a world that was complete, but human activity has upset the balance of the natural world — God's world. We are called to sustain ourselves and God's world. This once, but no longer, "complete" world needs us to place sustainability among the value systems that we aspire to. If humans can adapt to a changing world the way religion has adapted, we will be on our way to a sustainable society.

The Circle of Simplicity

by Cecile Andrews

CECILE ANDREWS, who regards herself as the hedonist of the Simplicity Movement, wrote *Circle of Simplicity: Return to the Good Life* and *Slow is Beautiful: New Visions of Community, Leisure, and Joie de Vivre*. She is a founder of an urban community called Phinney Ecovillage. She holds a doctorate in education from Stanford University.

MANY YEARS AGO, I was introduced to a young man who seemed vaguely familiar. In trying to establish where we'd met, he said, "Aren't you the person who talks about the 'self-deprivation' movement?"

How to respond? "Yes, that's me!"

But of course he had it exactly wrong! Simplicity makes your life more enjoyable, more fun.

For years, I've tried to communicate the joys of Simplicity. But not long ago, another young man made me want to throw in the towel. While visiting our home, he read the notes on our refrigerator and noticed the grocery list that I had just started. "Wow," he said. "You really walk your talk!"

"What?!" I responded. I came over and looked at the list. There were only two items: bread and water. "No," I cried.

"It's not what it looks like! It's not my week's rations! This is organic bread and mineral water for a party."

Too many times, I've had responses like this. Americans are drawn to Simplicity, yet at the same time they fear it. Certainly, no one wants a life of deprivation, but many of us have come to understand that *less can be more*.

Less is more. A jarring statement to Americans who have been taught that more is always better. But we know this approach to life hasn't worked. No need to list the many American emotions — depression, anxiety, hostility, fear, anger, lust, disdain, envy, resentment.

Yet we elected Barack Obama. When we had a more positive alternative, we chose it. It's the same with the idea of Simplicity. Americans are drawn to it, and if we understand it, I think we will choose it.

It's a basic idea found in all religions and wisdom traditions: On one level, Simplicity is about limiting your outer wealth so you can have inner wealth. History, research and our life experience have shown that if you focus on outer riches then you won't have inner riches. It just doesn't work.

But there's another way to look at Simplicity. It's making conscious choices. It's choosing freely instead of being manipulated. I think of it as "the examined" life, a life in which we look at the consequences of our behaviors in terms of the well-being of people and the planet. It's making conscious choices about what's important and what matters. It's stripping away the inessential so the essential shines through.

Many of us have experienced for ourselves the idea that "less is more." We have limited our outward accumulation of stuff so that we find more fulfillment in our lives. By limiting the acquisitive side of our lives, our inner lives have grown. Most of us consume less so that we have time to pursue our personal passions. If we spend less, we can work less. If we have less stuff, we spend less time on stuff. It takes time to buy stuff, to manage stuff, to fix stuff. Everything seems to break down these days. You know what I mean.

People choosing Simplicity make a lot of different changes. I quit my full-time job as a community college administrator and became a community educator — writing, teaching and working to develop community and sustainability in my neighborhood. To many that sounds risky. But who feels more secure? The person who earns little, and therefore lives on less and makes sure not to rack up debt, or the person who gets a high salary, buys lots of things, goes into debt and then loses his or her job.

One of the benefits of living more simply is that no one has high expectations of you. No one expects me to have a remodeled kitchen. No one expects much from my wardrobe. If I seem to wear the same clothes all the time, people think I'm acting on principle, not just lack of fashion sense! My life is much more free of the anxiety of meeting others expectations. And certainly I'll never feel like I'm a failure, because I've never accepted society's definition of success!

What Simplicity has brought me most is clarity. Inner clarity. It's wonderful to know what I believe, what I think, what my values are. When one woman noticed that I was, once again, forming another community group, she said, "You must have been a sheepdog in a former life." I thought, "Yes! It's so nice to know your essential self!"

But clarity comes from deliberation. This is the most essential ingredient of Simplicity. It's taking time to think, asking yourself what you want. As Thoreau said in *Walden*, "I went to the woods because I wished to live deliberately… and not, when I came to die, discover that I had not lived." We're choosing the deliberate life of Simplicity because it makes us feel fully alive.

How do we feel fully alive? By making a difference. In living simply, we make a difference: the survival of our planet depends on our using fewer resources. The well-being of poor people depends on our living more simply. As Americans use fewer resources, we'll no longer excite the wrath of other peoples, and the world will be safer from terrorism.

It's clear then, that if we care about the well-being of people and the planet, we need to change. Some respond that Simplicity will destroy the economy. But excuse me? Who destroyed the economy? The people who think consciously and carefully about their money? I don't think so. Simplicity didn't hurt the economy. Unprincipled, unregulated greed did.

So, what do we need to do to live simply? Ultimately, we must challenge our basic American belief system about money. Why? Because it is our belief system about money that causes so many of our problems. There are two beliefs: One, that being rich makes you happy. (All the research says that after a certain point it doesn't.) And two, that if you work hard enough — as most Americans believe — you'll be rich. Also false. As long as you believe those two things, you won't protest when the rich are getting tax cuts because you think that you could be one of the rich and that you would be happy! And then, the income gap continues to grow, creating a vicious cycle: as the wealthy gain more and more power, life becomes more cutthroat, and people strive even harder for more money.

As long as people believe that being rich is their goal, they will not only engage in corruption, they will accept it in others. It's greed and the pursuit of wealth that have caused corporations to cheat and lie. It's the hope for wealth that has caused the public to accept this.

The economic crisis of the fall of 2008 was clearly based on greed — the pursuit of wealth regardless of the ethics. As Thomas Friedman says in his November 25, 2008 *New York Times* column:

This financial meltdown involved a broad national breakdown in personal responsibility, government regulation and financial ethics.

So many people were in on it: People who had no business buying a home, with nothing down and nothing to pay for two years; people who had no business pushing such mortgages, but made fortunes doing so; people who had no business bundling those loans into securities and selling them to third parties, as if they were AAA bonds, but made fortunes doing so; people who had no business rating those loans as AAA, but made fortunes doing so; and people who had no business buying those bonds and putting them on their balance sheets so they could earn a little better yield, but made fortunes doing so.

It is clear that the pursuit of wealth changes you. It makes people more greedy and selfish. It's like an eating disorder. After young girls have dieted severely, engaging in bingeing and purging, they are incapable of eating in a sensible manner without outside help. This is what seems to happen to people pursuing wealth. They get greedier and greedier. They can't stop themselves. They need the outside help of laws and regulations.

So the research shows that the pursuit of wealth will not make you happy. However, there's another, related piece of research that is more compelling than any other: *The biggest predictor of the health of a nation, as measured in longevity, is the wealth gap. The bigger the gap, the lower everyone's longevity.* It's not just that poor people's health brings down the average. (Which is part of it, of course.) No, it hurts the wealthy as well. The rich person in this country doesn't have the longevity the middle-class person has in Norway, a country committed to a small wealth gap.

Why is this? It seems that a wealth gap destroys social cohesion. It creates a society in which people do not feel connected with others, do not feel responsible for others, do not care about the common good. When a society allows a wealth gap, it's telling people: It's a jungle out there. It's a cutthroat world. Do what you must in order to survive. Watch your back. Don't trust anyone. Don't expect any help. Don't expect fairness. It's every man for himself. You're on your own.

In this kind of society, people feel like they have to hustle constantly if they are to survive. They lie and cheat to get ahead. Crime and violence grow. Of course citizens come to believe that no one cares, that you can't trust anyone. Social cohesion is destroyed.

The resulting sense of isolation and lack of belonging takes its toll. But there's something more: Part of this is the inequality of status. There is something very harmful about inequality. The poorer people are forced to feel shame and envy. The rich people feel arrogance, contempt and disdain, as well as guilt and fear of reprisal. These are not healthy emotions! They're not good for you! Yes, it's more pleasant to have higher status, but the high-status person never really feels good because there's always someone higher! And when you're at the top, you know everyone is trying to dethrone you. And who likes those people at the top? Do they even like each other? No, they never know who will be the one to stick the knife in.

Ultimately, the greatest harm comes because no one feels part of something greater than themselves. You feel isolated, disconnected, ignored, abandoned and alone. Again, these emotions are bad for you! All the research shows that feelings of caring and connection lead to health, happiness and longevity. Anger, fear, resentment and loneliness are devastating to people. These emotions will only disappear as the wealth gap disappears. A country with a large and strong middle class is one in which government has stepped in to say that the important thing is the common good, not extreme profits for a few. People have long argued the "trickle-down" theory of economics. We have seen that it doesn't work.

What works is equality and connection — people understanding that our fate is tied to others' fate.

Now, how do we get to this kind of equality and connection? First, people must understand the truth: they must know that the United States, compared to European nations, is at the bottom or next to the bottom on things like happiness, equality, health, child welfare and voting. We're at the top in things like anti-depression medications, healthcare costs, homicide and incarceration. We don't have the "highest standard of living" if you measure it in terms of quality of life and well-being.

Citizens need to know that we work longer than any developed nation and that happiness is declining. They need to know that we have spent twice as much on health care as Europe, yet we're at the bottom of the health indicators. We need to educate the public about these facts. We need to work for policies that bring us greater equality, shorter work hours and a reduction in the use of oil.

But we can't do this with only an emphasis on the negative. We can't just evoke fear about our predicament. We need to find a way to awaken people to the excitement and fulfillment of Simplicity. I found a reference to a quotation from the author of *The Little Prince*, St. Exupery. He said that if he wanted a boat built, he wouldn't just give people a bunch of tools and wood; no, he would *teach them to yearn for the vast and endless sea*.

I love that. We must give people a vision of this new life, a vision that is so exciting and compelling that people will do everything they can to realize that vision. Instead of shaking our fingers at people for their consumerism, we must help them discover a way of life in which they lose the *desire* to consume. I found such a vision in the slow food movement, a movement that argues that we should be joining with friends and family for a long, leisurely, delicious meal with lots of conversation and laughter instead of eating tasteless fast food alone while we're watching television.

The slow food movement has swept around the world! People understand it intuitively. And of course it goes beyond the appeal of just a pleasant evening. This image of enjoyment is linked to environmental and social justice concerns. If you want good food, you need to pay attention to how it's grown. You need to pay attention to what corporate agriculture is doing to people and the planet.

As I thought about the success of the slow food movement, I realized that this is the vision that will motivate us. It's the basic vision of the good life: connection, caring and joy. The joyful community.

All the research makes clear that it's our relationships with others that are at the heart of happiness. When people are connected, caring and engaged, they're happier, healthier and live longer.

We Must Develop Community

On one hand, when you hear about the importance of community, you think, of course that's right. But in reality, it's at the bottom of people's lists. They not only don't have time for community, they really don't think it's very important. Or, they think they're experiencing community when they go to the mall or watch a rerun of *Friends*.

To inspire people to work for community, we "teach them to yearn for the vast and endless sea" by giving them the experience of community, the experience of caring and being cared for. You only become more caring by being cared for. We do not feel cared for in this cutthroat culture. You learn to compete, to achieve, to prove you're better than others; you judge others, compare yourself to others; you learn to ignore the homeless, to hide your real feelings with a false image; you learn to cheat, to fool people, to trick them, to manipulate them. Who doesn't worry they will end up alone, abandoned and neglected — sitting drugged in a wheelchair, warehoused with other old people.

Aldous Huxley called it "organized lovelessness." We choose technology over people and interact more and more with machines — voice mail, e-mail, cash machines. We even check our own library books outs. You don't need anyone and no one needs you.

But look at what people throughout history have said:

Heroes are not giant statues framed against a red sky. They are people who say: This is my community, and it is my responsibility to make it better. Interweave all these communities and you really have an America that is back on its feet again. I really think we are gonna have to reassess what constitutes a "hero."

— STUDS TERKEL

What should young people do with their lives today? Many things, obviously. But the most daring thing is to create stable communities in which the terrible disease of loneliness can be cured.

— KURT VONNEGUT, JR.

When the stranger says: "What is the meaning of this city? Do you huddle together because you love one another?" What will you answer? "We all dwell together to make money from each other," or "This is a community"?

— T.S. ELIOT

Creating Community

When you experience community, you learn to care for people outside your own circle of friends and family. You learn to care for the "other." It's only in learning to care for others that you care for the common good, the greater good of society.

We must create new community groups as they are doing in the relocalization movement. We must support local businesses and join neighborhood councils. But those aren't enough. We must make community part of *everything* we do. When we have our meetings to talk about lobbying the city council, we need to start with tea and cookies and time to chat. Instead of ruthlessly pursuing Roberts Rules of Order, we need someone who runs the meetings in a relaxed, conversational manner allowing people to talk of their personal experiences. Interspersed with meetings to save the trees, we need potlucks and picnics where people gather in a congenial, convivial fashion. We need meetings about global warming, but we also need Scrabble nights. We need to donate money to political campaigns, but we also need to stop and chat with our neighbors.

Because ultimately, without community, we won't learn to share or care. If we don't learn to care about our own species, maybe we can't care about other species. Caring is a human ability that needs to be nurtured and developed if it is to thrive.

And community will only thrive if it's in a culture that values Simplicity, knowing that less is more.

Simplicity today, then, is about much more than cutting back on your clothes allowance or forgoing a kitchen remodel. It's about creating a culture of connection in which people feel cared for. This will come about when we challenge our belief system about money. This will happen when we create community groups. This will happen when we learn to hang out with each other in local coffee shops. We will only believe in the welfare of people and planet when we have experienced caring and connection. Throughout human history, there have been big changes. At one time, most people believed that slavery was acceptable. They believed in the divine right of kings. They believed that torture was acceptable. We can change our belief system about money by creating a culture of Simplicity.

Like Corn in the Night: Reclaiming a Sense of Time

by Rebecca Kneale Gould

REBECCA KNEALE GOULD is the author of *At Home in Nature: Modern Homesteading and Spiritual Practice in America*. An associate professor of Religion and Environmental Studies at Middlebury College, she teaches courses on religion and nature, environmental ethics, religion and social change in America and Simplicity in American culture. Her current research is on religiously informed environmental activism. Rebecca is an enthusiastic board member of Take Back Your Time. Her latest Simplicity venture is being a Boutique Shepherd. Together with her partner, Cynthia Smith, she is caring for three sheep in her modest, but graze-able backyard.

I WOULD LIKE TO BEGIN with one of my favorite passages from Thoreau's *Walden*. It appears in the "Sounds" chapter of the book, relatively early in the text, just after a long discourse on the virtues of reading. After describing the significant works that his fellow Concordians *must* read — as well as sketching a map of his own literary intentions — Thoreau abruptly shifts gears. "I did not read books the first summer," he allows, "I hoed beans." "Nay, I often did better than this." He goes on:

There were times I could not afford to sacrifice *the bloom of the present moment* to any work whether of the head or the hands. I love a broad margin to my life. Sometimes, in a summer morning, having taken my accustomed bath, I sat in my sunny doorway from sunrise until noon, rapt in a reverie, amidst the pines and hickories and sumacs, in undisturbed solitude and stillness, until … [by] the noise of some traveler's wagon I was reminded of the lapse of time. I grew in those seasons like corn in the night, and they were far better than any work of the hands would have been. They were not time subtracted from my life, but so much over and above my usual allowance.… For the most part, I minded not how the hours went. The day advanced as if to light some work of mine; it was morning and lo, now it is evening and nothing memorable is accomplished.[1]

This passage often brings tears to my eyes when I read it. Tears of recognition, of knowing what such moments can be like — of what it truly can mean to grow like corn in the night, because you have actually paused to allow yourself to do so. And tears emerging sometimes from a sense of loss, not only the personal loss that comes from being too busy to breath deeply (the default stance for most of us), but also a deeper sense of loss, that our American culture, defined as it is primarily by the valuation of consumption and relentless "doing," is a culture that does not sustain the kind of growth Thoreau is talking about — the growth that comes from doing nothing.

I've had an intellectual love affair with Thoreau since I was very young, and this love affair was rekindled (if, indeed, it had ever died out!) when a series of scholarly hunches and happy circumstances brought me into the orbit of Helen Nearing and, by extension, her late husband, the socialist, radical economist and pacifist, Scott Nearing. The Nearings also were lovers of Thoreau, and his two-year experiment at Walden was one of their inspirations when they left a cold-water flat in New York City in 1932 and, in stages, established themselves on a largely self-sufficient homestead in Southern Vermont.

I was drawn to study the Nearings' lives both before and after they began homesteading, in part because I wanted to know what "going back to nature" meant for those who took up the homesteading challenge for longer than Thoreau's two years (for the Nearings, it was over 50). And as my study expanded, so too did the cast of characters I brought into the orbit of my analysis. I reached back in history to John Burroughs, the first post-Thoreauvian homesteader who left a blossoming literary life in Washington, DC in the mid-19th century and returned to the geography of his childhood to create an interwoven livelihood of farming, writing and simple living along the Hudson. I also ventured forward into the present, interviewing particularly those homesteaders of today who have been inspired by the Nearings (and who often, also, find their muse in Thoreau).

The book that emerged from this study, *At Home in Nature*, asked questions about what it means to take the problem of meaning and the problem of living seriously. What has prompted urban and suburban dwellers to lay down old lives and take up new, fairly self-sufficient ones, growing their own food, building houses from wood cut onsite, producing a variety of homegrown cash crops (from vegetables to books) all in order to live a more proximate relationship with nature? The stories that homesteaders told about their lives were stories that often served as conversion narratives, and the rituals of daily homesteading practice, it became apparent to me, were not only practical, but also deeply spiritual. Building a house by hand or carrying water from a well every day served as ways of ritualizing a particular relationship to place, emphasizing intimacy with and respect for the natural world. These practices also simultaneously served as symbolic gestures of dissent from the excesses of American culture, particularly the culture of consumption.

But lurking behind the primary arguments of the text is a theme that I want now to emphasize, a theme so often not addressed in the growing conversations about "sense of place." It is one of taking back *time* from institutions that try to possess it. It is of daring to do nothing, or — if you are like the Nearings, who almost never did nothing — of insisting on doing an eclectic, pragmatic, yet artistic variety of *somethings*, but on a schedule of one's *own*, attuned to bursts of creativity, to the daily necessity of cutting wood for the fire or of harvesting and eating according to what the seasons demand. As Helen used to put it, "There is something extravagant and irresponsible about eating strawberries in January." When I first heard this comment, I was a bit put off: I found it quite ascetic and demanding. But now, although my own gardening and eating practices are never quite as pure, I understand more fully what she means. Eating in line with the seasons is eating on *nature's time*, not on culture's consumptive clock. No wonder that the kale we harvested from our garden this week tastes so sweet. We ate in step with the heartiness of kale in autumn, in step with the November frosts that kiss the bitterness off of the leaves.

In a sense, choosing to homestead and to live by nature's principles, means *taking the time* to know what those principles *are*. While the homesteaders I interviewed demonstrated a range of approaches to time, from pursuing project-filled days with intensity to inscribing carefully guarded "open time" into their homestead plan, many expressed a sense that the way "time" is conceptualized —

and acted on — in American culture is as problematic as the other aspects of mainstream culture that they were criticizing: the culture of unchecked materialism and of the attendant ecological destruction that results. For instance, John Burroughs articulated a sense of time quite similar to that of Thoreau (from whom he borrowed many ideas). Taking his cues from both Thoreau and from his friend Walt Whitman, Burroughs often spoke of the virtues of hours spent walking, walking to do errands and walking just for walking's sake. He felt it vitally important, he wrote, to "loaf and invite my soul."

One of the most inspiring aspects of the Nearings' book *Living the Good Life*, both aspiring homesteaders and interested readers alike have informed me, is their careful outlining of a daily pattern of living that allowed for new constructions of time. Early in their descriptions of homesteading life, the Nearings presented a model of living by which they spent a half day for bread labor (production of food for themselves and a cash crop [maple sugar] for the market) and a half day for personal pursuits, including, they reported, sunbathing and music-making. As their obligations and popularity grew, however, the Nearings also found themselves struggling with time. They needed to balance publishing their writing, keeping the gardens thriving and hosting increasing numbers of pilgrims who saw the Nearings' lives as "free" in a way that theirs were not and so, in seeking inspiration to live more sanely, ironically squeezed the very time and space that their role models had fought so hard to attain.

But despite the Nearings' own experiences of an overflowing schedule, their to-do list is still rather different. In reading their work, one gets a sense of the deep satisfaction that comes from their ability to shape time on their own terms and on the terms of the seasons of the year and the needs of the day, not on the demands (or whims) of a boss, an office or an executive board. The Nearings meditated, often gathered seaweed for the compost in silence, used hand tools rather than power tools and gardened deliberately, attentively. Of course the Nearings cultivated a "sense of place" — as did Thoreau, as did Burroughs — but they knew that nurturing a sense of time was equally crucial. Indeed, without time there really *is* no place. In the absence of time, place — which comes into being through memory and relationship — flattens into mere location. Outside the Maine homestead where I first met Helen, a simple blue wooden sign sat perched on a large boulder at the driveway. "Our mornings are our own. We'll see visitors 3–5," the sign read, "Help us lead the good life."

Homesteaders' lives show us clearly what our dominant culture is lacking. But if we step back from homesteading itself, we have some larger questions to ask. Homesteaders have dared to be artists of their own lives and to recreate themselves on terms that are closer to nature and further away from the dominant culture. All to the good. Homesteaders are determined and strong-minded people who have taken the risks (and often have some means of support) that enable them to radically reshape their lives. But what about the rest of us: the ones with "regular" jobs, kids to support, promotions to achieve? The most fatal aspect of our loss of time in North American culture, to my mind, is the extent to which this problem gets *privatized*. We think there is something wrong with *us*, we think we need to get better at time management, or that there is something severely lacking in our psychological makeup if we often feel overwhelmed. The problem of time famine in our culture — a phenomenon deeply intertwined with our patterns of consumption, unchecked individualism and ecological neglect — is not simply a "personal problem," it is also a social and cultural problem. And it is a problem that has to be *named*. For my purposes here, the act of naming involves first looking at the effects that emerge when overwork and time famine become dominant cultural norms. To my mind, the most significant effects are: overconsumption, the unraveling of family life, environmental degradation and a sharp decline in human health. Let me give a window on to each of these problems in turn.

Overconsumption

Juliete Schor has noted that, over the past 30 years, real consumption expenditures per person have *doubled* from $11,171 to $22,152 (adjusted for inflation). Her analysis reveals a double-edged sword that has emerged particularly in the 1980s and 90s:

> [The] booming economy reinforced a powerful cycle of "work and spend" in which consumer norms accelerated dramatically. People needed to work more to purchase all the new products being churned out by a globalizing consumer economy. And they responded to their stressful lives by participating in an orgy of consumer upscaling.[2]

While consumption may decline in leaner economic times, as is the case now at the end of the first decade of the millennium, Americans' history of out-consuming every other nation is likely not to change dramatically, even if we think it should. While there are multiple factors that influence high consumption rates, lack of time plays a role in many of them, from buying "quick-fix" products and services to help you do what you once could do yourself to purchasing expensive toys for children in lieu of spending the time (which you don't have) to walk and converse with them.

Family Life

The problem of overwork has a deleterious effect on the life and health of American families. A national poll of teenagers, funded by the White House in 2000, "found that over one-fifth rated 'not having enough time with parents' as their top concern, a percentage that tied for first (along with education) on their list of worries."[3]

Yet the unavailability of parents is often ironically tied to the encouragement of similar levels of uncontrolled busyness among kids who are slotted into piano lessons, soccer teams and school newspaper meetings such that they are never home either, a phenomenon that many argue comes in part from parents' guilt that they are not at home and their hope that their children will not "miss out on opportunities" as a result. Much research has been done on the "hurried child," and that research shows that while *some* structured time is an important alternative to sitting at home in front of the TV, a procession of nine-year-olds with date books under their arms is not promising either for the children's own lives or for our culture at large. Being a child who can no longer wander around in the neighborhood woods can lead not only to "nature deficit disorder" but also to an inability to engage creatively with time and space on one's own terms.

Environment

A study by the psychologist Tim Kasser, *The High Price of Materialism*, has shown that the ecological footprint of an individual (measured as the number of acres necessary to support one's chosen lifestyle) increases steadily in proportion to number of hours worked per week, and rises dramatically for those working more than 35 hours per week. Kasser showed that, at the same time that ecological footprints go up, genuine life satisfaction goes down.[4]

Human Health

Repetitive stress injuries, sleep deprivation, psychological stress, obesity, lack of exercise, anxiety and depression are all quite dangerous individually, but they may also conspire to cause diabetes, heart disease or cancer. All of these illnesses are linked in some way to the culture of overwork. Dr. Suzanne Schweikert has noted, however, that there is a deep irony here that brings us back to some social and political questions that are broader than those of work hours alone. "Our desire to keep our health insurance benefits," she pointed out, "ties us to jobs that are bad for our health." [5]

What do we do with all of this data? There are many approaches to take including first looking within to ask what in our *own* lives we would like to reform. But we need to go beyond self-reflection and to dare to insert into our public life an honest and deliberate conversation about time. We need to *manifest* in our culture the crucial connections between the necessity of unstructured time and ecological health, and community vitality and the life of the spirit. On my own college campus, my students *ache* for time to think, or just to be. Yet they also admit that having too much free time can make them nervous, that they're not sure what they would do with themselves if they had it. To me, this paradox says much about our culture. Our promising young people have so internalized the American culture of busyness that while they often desperately want out, they also don't want to end up too far away from the American cultural norm. What would they do and who would they be without it?

The point is not that we should all become homesteaders who cultivate a special sense of place and time that most of us do not or cannot have. The point is how to put public pressure to the urgent problem of time famine in way that supports private choices, but also directly addresses social structures. For what good is it if our minds are free to imagine a "broad margin to our lives," but our bodies and souls must stick to the narrow path that our workplaces, or our governments have cut for us? In my view, naming the problem — and insisting that it is *not* merely a personal problem but also an urgent social and cultural problem — is a good place to start.

And then, we get to work, giving voice to our need to nurture those dimensions of ourselves that are not *just* about efficiency and accomplishment. Few of us desire to leave our jobs behind — in many cases, we love them — but we *do* want to do them differently. My partner is a physician who wants to see patients in more than the insurance-mandated 15-minute slots, who wants to hear the whole story and know the whole person who comes in with a failing lung. And I am a professor who longs to be able to meet with each of my students for an hour a week — or even a month — to hear what they are really thinking about and what effects their classes are having on their lives — but that consultation time alone, would take up 50 hours. Most days, we don't want to ditch our work; we just want the time *for* doing our work in a richly human, fully present manner. And then there's our desire to get outdoors, to get out the vote, to recycle two years' worth of magazines, to truly observe a Sabbath. Exercise, nature, civic life, environmental health and spiritual life all shrink in the face of the goblin *no time*.

And yet we can do it. We can make taking back our time a public conversation and a public movement. Indeed, we are already beginning to do so. If we continue to give voice to what so many wish to keep silent, we can — like Thoreau — grow like corn in the night.

Simplicity, Simply Put

by Tom Turnipseed

TOM TURNIPSEED is an attorney, writer and political and
civil rights activist residing in Columbia, SC. Tom is also
a former state senator who has founded and led environmental and consumer groups. He has hosted several
radio and television shows that featured a variety of issues and interesting individuals with a particular emphasis on political and social satire.

WE CONSUME more of nature's resources than we need.
Our bad behavior is simply destroying life as we
know it in our ecosystem. We are simply killing ourselves
and our system of life with our greed. What will be left for
our children, grandchildren and future generations? Our
species is committing ecocide. Simple living can reduce
ecocide.

My wife Judy and I became involved in the Voluntary
Simplicity movement after attending an interactive lecture by John de Graaf at the University of South Carolina
ten years ago. After conversing with John and viewing his
award-winning documentary *Affluenza* on PBS, we became convinced that Simplicity is the cure for the runaway
greed created mainly by media advertising and its mindless
conditioning of targeted consumers. Since then we have

attended conferences on Voluntary Simplicity in Oberlin, Ohio, Seattle, Washington, and Chicago, Illinois.

We need to use simple words so people everywhere can understand these simple truths and stop destroying life. We must spread the word in simple language about these simple truths. Simple language is used on *The Seed Show*, our week-day morning drive-time radio show in Columbia, South Carolina, that I host. It begins with the refrain of "Sowing the Seeds of Love" by Tears for Fears, and we repeat each day that we are sowing the seeds of love, peace and justice and respect for everyone, everywhere in the world. Then we say if we really did think of all people in every culture on our globe as friends and neighbors we could have a much better chance to achieve such peace, justice and respect. Friends and neighbors and peace, justice and respect can be translated into every language and these simple words mean the same thing to people in every culture.

A language barrier exists between the intellectuals and academics who abound in the Voluntary Simplicity move-ment and the everyday working-class people who use simple and direct speech. The tendency to employ multi-syllabic words and abstractions in extended conversations and dis-sertations is pleasing to like-minded sophisticates involved in Voluntary Simplicity. But for everyday folks whose in-volvement is necessary if the Simplicity movement is to achieve its public policy goals that benefit all the people, it often comes across as highfalutin and condescending and is misunderstood. We must do better at using simple language because the goals of the Voluntary Simplicity movement in the US are critically important.

Further, it is time for the Simplicity movement to prog-ress beyond the voluntary acts of the more affluent and aca-demically affected. The importance of simple living gaining understanding and acceptance among people everywhere has never been more urgent. Simple living is the solution to the unprecedented ecological crisis of global warming and climate change caused by excessive and extravagant human activity.

Our greed-driven economy relies too much on oil and other fossil fuels — which create carbon dioxide (CO_2) in the atmosphere — that provide 80 to 85 percent of our energy. Too much carbon in the air causes global warming, contributing to more extreme weather, rising sea levels, changing precipitation patterns, ecological and agricultural dislocations and the increased spread of human disease, according to leading climatologists throughout the world. It is ecocidal when US policymakers fail to support global initiatives such as the Kyoto Accords.

Worldwide weather is becoming more extreme, and the habitat of all forms of life is being destroyed by our ecocidal species. Higher levels of CO_2 have already caused ocean acidification, and scientists are warning of potentially devastating effects on marine life and fisheries. An article outlining the impact of this destruction, published in 2004 in the science journal *Nature*, was co-authored by 18 eminent scientists from the US and UK. These researchers worked independently in six biodiversity-rich regions around the world and concluded that global warming will doom a million species by 2050. The arctic ice cap keeps melting more rapidly under the effects of global warming and in August 2008 saw its second-largest summer shrinkage since satellite observations began 30 years ago, according to US scientists at the National Snow and Ice Data Center. Simply put, people are burning too much oil and coal.

One issue that is hard even for Simplicity advocates to face is travel. Even people involved in the Voluntary Simplicity movement are too much into world travel and are leaving giant carbon footprints. They are a much larger contributing cause of global warming than necessary. Among the attendees at Voluntary Simplicity conferences are many academics whose travel expenses are usually paid by grants or their institutions. At a Voluntary Simplicity meeting at Oberlin, Ohio, several participants commented on their latest carbon-consuming trips abroad. I questioned our carbon footprints since most of us had come long distances in big jets. Such trivial travel talk with my friends in the Voluntary Simplicity movement brought back memories of the globe-trotting lifestyle of the very rich.

Traveling the globe and observing things first-hand gives a privileged few a personal look at what is going on in areas of the world they visit. But numerous nature channels and documentaries bring the wonders of life around the globe to our homes with stunningly vivid videography. And, with personal computers, we now have the natural world virtually at our finger tips, available for viewing in our own homes without leaving ecocidal carbon footprints. I am fascinated by faraway places with strange sounding names when I view photos and read about them in periodicals like *National Geographic* and newspapers such as the *New York Times*.

We need to encourage stay-close-to-home vacations, or "stay-cations", and check out nature's splendor, recreational opportunities and entertainment attractions nearby. Here in South Carolina, spokesmen for state agencies that promote tourism, such as our Department of Parks, Recreation and Tourism and the Department of Natural Resources, are regular guests on our radio show and are encouraging stay-cations to cope with the soaring cost of gasoline and reduce our carbon footprints. While we work hard to get legislation passed for paid stay-cations for exhausted Americans, we should look to bulls and bears as nature's symbols for guidance.

A charging bull was the strutting symbol of once-mighty Merrill-Lynch, the vaunted brokerage house whose shocking financial failure ended with its demise and takeover by Bank of America, and a bull market is the symbol of making big money. Perhaps a more bearish market would have a positive effect and help move us toward true Simplicity. To be bearish is to know we must have time for nature. That is Simplicity, simply put.

Enroute to Eldertown: Where Fast Lanes Turn into Pastures and Meadows

by Theodore Roszak

THEODORE ROSZAK has written 15 works of non-fiction, including the 1969 classic, *The Making of a Counter Culture*, its recently published "sequel," *The Making of an Elder Culture*, and five novels. He was educated at UCLA and Princeton and has taught at Stanford, the University of British Columbia, San Francisco State University and the State University of California, East Bay. He and his wife and occasional co-author, Betty, live in Berkeley, California.

THE NEWS OF THE DAY — and for that matter the history of the 20th century — gives every good reason to despair for the future of our society. And yet, as bleak as things may seem, there are other forces in play — subtle, long-term undercurrents that are shaping our lives for the better even if we cannot always see them at work. One of these, and I believe it is the most consequential but least appreciated force of all, is the demographic transition usually called the longevity revolution. That more people are living

79

longer is common knowledge, the subject of all the television snippets about pension plans, health care and fitness that fill in the last five minutes of the network news. What is less recognized is how deeply rooted our lengthening life expectancy is in the history of modern times, that it is indeed so inevitable a development that it deserves to be seen as the biological and spiritual destiny of our species.

The longevity revolution is a cultural sea change that does not depend on the brilliant insights of a few gifted minds, less still on organized movements or the charisma of a great leader. It is more like an environmental than a political transformation. Indeed, I believe it may be the planetary ecology finding a way to protect its cargo of life from a runaway industrial system.

As a history teacher, I have often pondered the fact that, throughout the past, the people I have been studying were born to a lifespan of some 50 years. By the time they reached 45, they were old. Some lived to be very old, but not many. When old-age pensions were first established in Europe and the United States, the retirement age was arbitrarily set at 65 by political leaders who knew that most people would never live to collect the money. That in itself — the sense of how much time one has left to work out one's salvation — changes everything about the way one makes choices, about one's hopes and ambitions.

In its youth, the boomer generation discovered the politics of consciousness transformation. "You say you want a revolution.... Well, you know, we all want to change your head." I had students during the sixties and seventies who were dosing on anything that was rumored to be psychedelic, every herb, plant and industrial chemical they could lay their hands on that might allow them to explore some purportedly higher level of awareness. But the greatest consciousness-transforming agent of all comes to us from within our own experience and as naturally as breathing. It is the experience of aging, which brings with it new values and visions, none of them grounded in competition and careerism, none of them beholden to the marketplace.

It may be that the old have always realized that you can't take it with you, but their numbers were never great enough, their voice never strong enough to make them a decisive factor in society; nor did they expect to live long enough to lend their insight any social importance. Now, in ever greater numbers, we are aging beyond the values that created the urban–industrial world. That fact begins with the boomers, but it will roll forward into generations to come as the now-young become the then-old — and live longer and longer. Which means that every institution in our society will be transformed as its population drifts further and further from competitive individualism, military–industrial bravado and the careerist rat race. It is as if the freeways of the world will one day soon begin to close down, starting with the fast lane and finally turning into pastures and meadows.

And with that change in personal life, we can begin to see a subtle wave of ecological change that will help us rein in the worst excesses of commercialism, consumerism and environmental damage. Life in "Eldertown" will be nothing like the worldwide urban ethos of freeways, sprawling suburbs, shopping malls and gas-guzzling cars. The elder culture will find little reason to uproot forests, pollute the seas and strip-mine the Earth. To be sure, on its own, the ecology of aging will not take effect rapidly, surely not soon enough to save many environmental treasures. But that is not what I expect. Rather, I believe there will come a time within this century, perhaps before the boomer generation leaves the scene, when we begin to recognize that, by working along the grain of the longevity revolution and the changes it brings about in our everyday values, we can achieve an environmentally enlightened social order.

The most important line of demarcation in contemporary politics may have to do with one's vision of history. Where do we stand as a society in the turbulent flow of events? Conservative thinkers believe a good dose of unrestrained entrepreneurial energy will solve all problems. Others, myself included, believe that urban–industrial society is playing out its endgame. It has arrived at a boundary condition where more of the same will not save us. Beyond that boundary lies either a downward spiral into economic and environmental chaos — or a new post-industrial world whose guiding ideas and inspiring ideals will be very different from those we have been following for the past three centuries. Issues of this magnitude cannot be settled by a few statistics. They are matters of philosophical commitment based on what we have learned about people, their vices, their virtues, their resourcefulness and, above all, their moral wisdom.

Throughout the modern era, Western society has looked to its ability to redesign nature for security and prosperity, just as the nations of the Western world once looked to war to achieve national greatness. We have been living out a Faustian bargain, a love affair with power: the power of our monkey cunning, the power of brute force. We have spent several generations beating our fellow human beings and the natural world into submission: native peoples, slaves, the working class, the land, the rivers, the forests, everything from the backward billions of our own species down to the microbes and the molecules of living systems. Perhaps our insatiable appetite for power made sense as long as human beings lived in helpless fear of famine, plague and the annihilating forces of nature. But industrial and scientific power has served its purpose; it has given us more than we need, so much, in fact, that we are running out of space to bury the excess and out of time to repair the damage. Dr. Faust may still have wonders and amazements up his sleeve, but we can no longer assume they will bring us more blessings than liabilities. The Simplicity and innocence of our quest for domination has come to an end. Something new, something that goes beyond power and plenty, must take its place as the goal of history — something that has to do with finding a greater meaning for human life than shopping sprees and space shots.

My experience of the sixties left me with no clear idea what that "something" might turn out to be, but I knew it had to do with questioning the rightness and rationality of urban–industrial society. That was a question none of the major ideologies of the past had ever dared to raise. On both the political left and right, capitalists, Marxists and socialists were committed to expanding the empire of cities that now girdles the Earth. All were convinced that industrial power was the whole meaning of progress, the only defensible way to use our skills and resources. All that mattered was who ran the system. "More" — more merchandise, more profit, more growth — "more" of everything was the goal of life, and technology was the means to that goal. Alongside that pursuit, everything else was defunct, irrational, backward.

This was the culture I saw being challenged in the sixties by the voices of a new generation. Eventually, the term "counterculture" took on a life of its own, usually becoming more superficial and purely sensational as it was passed along. Often it was understood to have more to do with hairstyles or ragged jeans or light shows. Definitions like that did not have to be trivial; the counterculture did express itself in its peculiar taste in dance and music; it had its emblems and gestures. The motley, thrift-shop chic of the period was a celebration of cheap living and a rebuke to expensive mainstream fashions. But too often the values that underlay the emblems and gestures went unappreciated. At least for me, the deeper meaning of the counterculture surfaced in the literature, music and film that explored the meaning of sanity. *Catcher in the Rye*, *One Flew Over the Cuckoo's Nest*, *Catch 22*, *The Naked Lunch*, *Dr. Strangelove*, *The Bell Jar*, the beat poetry of the fifties, the acid rock of the sixties, the psychiatric theories of R. D. Laing and the Mad Liberation Front, the psychedelic art of the underground press — works like this probed the limits of the official reality principle. Even the satirical magazine *Mad* that went out to the teens and preteens of the period was premised on the craziness of the adult way of life. One has to return to the early Romantic period to find the same fascination with madness and what it reveals. The boomers' early years were a time of protest, but the protest went beyond conventional political issues of justice, equality and peace. At its most radical, it took its politics to the depths of the psyche. Change consciousness and you change the culture. Change the culture and you change values. Change values and you change politics. That was the counterculture I cared about. The manifesto that spoke to me was Shelley's proclamation: "Poets are the unacknowledged legislators of the world."

Now, as I look back, I can see how difficult it was to formulate such a critique in political terms, especially when those who sought to do so were as young and frequently as gauche as boomers then were. Challenging the values of urban–industrial culture requires more experiential depth than one can expect from the very young. The project of transforming perceptions and values still seems to me the way forward toward a humane society, but this cannot be done with push-button rapidity by jolting the nervous system, whether with drugs or very, *very* loud music. Rather, it is best done by moving with the grain of nature.

Life in its normal course alters our consciousness more than any narcotic, especially if we are given the chance to reflect on our experience. The greatest transformations any of us undergo arise out of the rhythms of ordinary life: the trauma of birth, the trials of adolescence, suffering serious disease, facing the loss of loved ones, confronting our own death. Aging turns many of us into totally different people. If we confront the experience with full awareness, aging can prepare us to learn what so many great sages have tried to teach: to be mindful of our mortality, to honor the needs of the soul, to practice compassion. Conscious aging opens us to these truths; it is a mighty undoer of the ego. It sweeps away the illusions that once made wealth and competitive success, good looks and fine possessions, seem so important. Granted, age comes hard to some, especially a certain class of alpha male who may never find his way to wisdom because he can never give up on the rat race, never cease pursuing the glittering prizes, never stop doing battle with the young guys coming along. Granted, too, there are any number of old fools in the world. Just as youth can be wasted on the young, age can be wasted on the old. But was anybody who turns out to be a fool at 70 any wiser at the age of 20? At this crux in our history, my faith goes out to our countercultural capacities, meaning our ability to change course. Once I pegged that faith to what a big younger generation might be able to achieve. Now I would look to what a big older generation is far more likely to achieve, not simply on the basis of high ideals, but working along the grain of demographic necessity.

Once again, I remind myself that nothing good or bad is guaranteed in history. The world will always turn out to be what most of us make of it. But there are moments in time when possibilities present themselves and we must take our chances. I believe the new beginning that boomers fell short of achieving in their youth has become more possible and more practical with every year we have added to our life expectancy — a prospect nobody could have predicted. We have arrived at this juncture thanks to the productivity of our technology and to the demographic shift that technology has helped bring about. *Urban–industrial culture is aging beyond the values that created it.* The revolution belongs to the old, not the young.

Others will disagree. They see the rise of the wrinklies as a disaster, a fiscal train wreck, a death blow to the prospects for progress. They see a world dominated by grandparent power as backward, stagnant and unaffordable, a society burdened to the point of bankruptcy by nursing homes and demented millions. Meanwhile, there are those in the biotech community who are doing all they can to extend our life expectancy by decades, if not centuries — seemingly with no regard for the larger consequences of what they do.

Perhaps the doomsayers will be correct. Perhaps it will turn out that way — though not because it has to. My own hope is that the boomers — the best educated, most widely traveled, most innovative generation we have ever seen — are not too frivolous to face the dilemmas of longevity. On the contrary. I believe they will, in growing numbers as the years unfold, recognize that the making of an elder culture is the great task of our time, a project that can touch life's later years with nobility and intellectual excitement.

[Note: Excerpted from *The Making of an Elder Culture*, New Society Publishers, 2009.]

PART TWO

Solutions

Introduction

by Cecile Andrews

Now that we've begun to understand what Simplicty is, what do people involved in the Simplicity movement do? As we've seen over and over, they reject the idea that being rich will make them happy. They understand that happiness comes from supportive relationships with other people, from a sense of purpose and enjoyment of your life. It comes from creating community and a caring society in which "we're all in this together."

The first step is the act of *deliberation and discernment*: Ask yourself what's important and what matters. It's taking time to ask yourself what gives you energy and a sense of joie de vivre. These are the ultimate questions. People practicing Simplicity take different paths, but they are paths that emerge from the uniqueness of each individual. Some may devote themselves to their work, cutting back on anything that is an obstacle; others may make leisure their goal. Most look for balance. But status isn't their goal. They don't pursue an empty careerism just so they'll be rich or become an "important" person. They consciously choose.

The second step is usually *reducing spending*. Once you *know* what you want, you're highly motivated to save your money so that you can *get* what you want. In fact, reducing consumerism is easy when you've discovered your particular passion, because you don't even want to go to the mall. Your life is just too interesting! Most people don't really know what they want, so they blindly accept advertisement's message that tells them to buy. Aimlessly spending money is what you do when you're confused about your life's direction. When you begin to think about your spending habits, you realize how cunningly our culture has tricked us into believing that if you have any desire, go out and shop. If you have any problems, spend some money. The centrality of money is deeply ingrained in us.

The third step is an *analysis of the idea of "balance."* Even if you have work you love, too much of it sours. All work and no play... people in the Simplicity movement want time for their family, for their community and for personal goals, as well as for work. And so they try to cut back on work hours, shopping, watching television and keeping up appearances.

People involved in Simplicity, then, always return to the issue of *deliberation*: thinking through how they can live the good life.

Today a life of Simplicity involves more than individuals escaping the materialistic values of mainstream society. It's about creating a new society based on community — especially local, neighborhood community.

This is the exciting new direction that the Simplicity Movement is taking. It's much less involved with lonely individualism and more committed to bringing people together and creating a culture of connection. People shop locally, patronize independent stores, join food co-ops, enroll in car-sharing clubs and frequent farmers' markets. They visit local garage sales. They rent out rooms in their house, or join co-housing and ecovillages. They create neighborhood organizations and hang out in local coffee houses. When they travel, they exchange homes, volunteer at organic farms or "couch surf" (staying free in people's homes around the world, and agreeing to host people yourself).

All of these activities not only save you money and reduce the use of resources, they also bring you in closer connection with other people! Ultimately, without community we cannot live sustainably. When we live in community, we share more — we don't all need to have our own houses, cars, tools, etc. When you hang out in your local coffee shop, you don't have to drive across the city or to the mall for your entertainment.

But most of all, experiencing community helps you learn to *care*, a human ability that needs support and encouragement, but is too often discouraged and repressed by our consumer society. As you learn to care about the people in your neighborhood, maybe you're also learning to care for other species and for the well-being of people in poor countries. Community reduces the use of resources, but more than anything, it creates a culture of caring.

When people embrace Simplicity, their actions emerge from their uniqueness, so nobody does it the same way. But almost always, people consume less, work less and enjoy themselves more. And increasingly, they enjoy themselves in community.

Now, let us see what our authors do.

Simplicity Isn't "Voluntary" Any More

by Ernest Callenbach

ERNEST CALLENBACH's *Living Poor with Style* (still available in the abridged form, *Living Cheaply with Style*) was one of the first books to address how independence of mind could counter consumerist conformism and lead to elegant Simplicity. In his novels *Ecotopia* and *Ecotopia Emerging*, he depicted a future society in which everybody lived simply. He also wrote *Ecology: A Pocket Guide*.

I WROTE *Living Poor with Style* in the late sixties and early seventies. In those days, mostly in hopes of not appearing preachy, we spoke of Voluntary Simplicity as a way to escape the consumption rat race and leave time and energy for what we really wanted to do. We argued for simple living as a too little explored lifestyle choice, and it was. "Outwardly simple while inwardly rich" was a feasible alternative for many. In those days, young people could survive handily on half-time incomes, and half-time jobs were not too hard to find. (Sometimes they even came with benefits.) In those days, if you were observant and thoughtful and determined, you could live well on surprisingly small amounts of money — by keeping your attention on the quality of your life, not the quantity of your goods or the size of your disposable income. You could withdraw your emotional energy from work or consumption and devote it to love, spirituality, music or joining movements to improve the lot of your fellow citizens. In a pinch, you crashed with friends. You shared food, and beds, and wine or pot. You passed around clothes, from person to person or through "free boxes" of donated cast-offs. You could sometimes, with application and some luck, feel free of money entirely for days on end, and thus learn to put your attention on happier and more productive concerns.

Now we have entered a new era, in which Simplicity is not voluntary; it's being forced upon us. But the situation actually isn't all that new, though you wouldn't know it from the corporate media. Since the seventies, real incomes (the amount of bread you can buy with an hour of your labor) have remained static for huge numbers of Americans. As a people, we have *not* been "getting ahead." Part-time jobs have largely vanished, and full-time jobs have often become transient stopovers. Health coverage and pensions are vanishing for a large part of the population. Of the inexpensive nourishing foods we could once recommend (fish, peanut butter, rice, etc.), only beans and potatoes have remained truly affordable. In most areas where there are jobs, rents have grown to the point where even shared apartments or houses are a burden.

This was bad enough, but people made do. Their advertiser-driven cravings for small types of manufactured goods seemed satisfiable through the lower prices of Chinese-made stuff. Wives and husbands both worked, and they often took on second and sometimes third jobs. Family life and child upbringing suffered, but almost everybody was eating. (Eating too much, in fact — though overpackaged pseudo-food.)

But now, suddenly, things have taken a turn for the worse. The end of cheap oil (no doubt aided by speculators, but basically a consequence of world demand out-racing supply) is cranking up the price of everything that depends on petroleum, directly or indirectly. Most obviously, this means gas prices; we suddenly understand the real cost of dispersing our cities into vast environment-trashing suburban sprawl. But it also means food prices: modern agriculture pumps something like ten calories of fossil-fuel energy into every calorie of food energy; that delicious carrot you unthinkingly bite into is really mostly oil. And oil costs strongly affect the cost of the omnipresent plastics in everything from cars to drink containers.

Oil-based consumer industrialism is a game that cannot continue another generation. Oil-based food and oil-based trucking, shipping, air travel, along with oil-based home heating and cooling, and even fossil-fuel-driven information technology, will become so expensive that people can't even meet food bills. What happens then, we cannot guess, and some of the possibilities are very ugly. Some people hope for a soft landing, in which decline is gradual and perhaps manageable; in this scenario, the pain of costly oil will stimulate smart alternative-energy developments and more efficient energy usage in time to avert chaos. But many others anticipate a hard landing, marked by economic breakdowns, disintegration of institutions and widespread violence. We didn't foresee catastrophe and use our temporary oil wealth to forestall it.

But at the moment, wise Simplicity *can* help us cope. A life driven by consumption is not only an emotionally harried one, it's becoming economically impossible. We're shifting priorities — from toys to necessities. Instead of new shoes, we buy food. Instead of driving miles to find bargains in an outlet, we shop down the street and congratulate ourselves on coming out ahead anyway. Instead of looking for a house with thousands of square feet, we find an apartment that's just big enough and doesn't require a long car commute. Instead of buying an SUV, even a crossover one, we look for a gas-sipping small car and long for a plug-in hybrid. Or we begin to explore what life could be like without any car at all — using car-share companies, giving each other rides, carpooling, walking, bicycling, using the bus.

One silvery lining of such moves away from our petroleum-dependent habits is that they may teach us to get along better. Americans are famously individualistic. When the West was still empty, pioneers didn't even want to see the smoke from a neighbor's chimney. We want our *own* everything. The car and television and iPod are dominant technologies largely because they enable us to isolate ourselves from each other and interact with machines instead. But forced Simplicity (fewer goods, less mobility, less space and fewer choices generally) will motivate us to share, to cooperate, to understand each other's needs and priorities. To become little by little, in short, better people — in psychological and community and even religious terms — though not in economists' terms, where all that counts is transactions. And since happiness, researchers tell us, is more dependent on relationships than on goods, we may even end up happier.

When we can't be good, obedient solo consumers anymore, we may realize we have to take care of each other. That everybody's welfare matters, not just your own. That we need politicians and political institutions that are not for sale to the high bidders who provide campaigning funds, but people and structures (like "clean elections") that might actually help ordinary people out.

Economists like wealth. Because they imagine that economics determines everything, and they are ignorant of biology, they figure wealth and material growth will always find a way to counter the problems they create. They imagine that if our carbon dioxide emissions not only heat up the Earth but constrain the CO_2-absorbing ability of ocean organisms, we'll just find a way to do their job for them; technology will always save us, despite the end of cheap energy. Unfortunately, however, this argument is backward. Damage to the environment is closely proportional to wealth. The rich countries of the North, America and Europe and Japan, however many greenish companies they harbor, do far more damage than the poor countries of the South, though China and India are working hard to catch us in both production and consumption. But the underlying reality is inescapable: the richer you are, the more damage you do, no matter how fancy your technology, and ultimately that damage undermines your biological support systems and thus your own position of comfort and privilege.

A decline in real income, then, for people in the overdeveloped countries of the North (so far, mainly in the US), has ecological advantages along with horrendous personal costs for ordinary and poorer people. The question is, if we live simply and well, can it also have personal and social benefits? As was said long ago: "It is easier for a camel to go through the eye of a needle than for a rich man to enter the kingdom of God." Translating this into contemporary terms, unless we become poorer and smarter and live more simply, we confront ecological collapses that will end our hopes for an ecologically sustainable, equitable and happy future. But if we take advantage of our changing situation, we can turn less income and consumption into better lives.

Nobody would argue that lacking food, shelter and medical care should be acceptable to the citizens of any modern society. A humane government, such as we have not seen in the US for many years now, works to ensure that its or-

dinary citizens, not just the rich, can achieve minimally de-
cent lives. We need to exert every ounce of our strength as
citizens to enforce this goal upon every politician. Since the
only thing that truly moves politicians is fear, we need to
make them fear us at the ballot box more than they fear their
financial backers. As we organize to work on that, however,
it is up to us to make the best of our circumstances, and if
we pay responsive attention, there will be some surprising
liberatory sides to our changing times.

For one thing, in the more straitened era we have now
entered, buying choices will shrink. When you must use
all your disposable income for food, gas and medical care,
what does it matter that a supermarket offers 219 varieties
of sugar-laden breakfast cereal, or that overpriced running
shoes come in 16 colors? As sales of such supersaturated
market categories shrink, manufacturers will be forced to
produce fewer varieties within each category. Internet and
mail-order catalogs will decline both in number and in contents. In my opinion, at least, this will be a relief, because
consumption choices consume our time and our mental
energy. They often do not really pay off in satisfaction
when we have finally made up our minds and put down our
money. And goods themselves can be an energy sink; we
buy them thinking they will make us happy, and then find
they lay obligations on us — to pay them off, to learn how to
work them, to protect them from kids and pets, to find repair service for them when they break down and to dispose
of them safely when they no longer work or we have grown
sick of them.

Having less disposable cash to buy things, and fewer
choices among goods available, we will be forced to concen-
trate on choices that don't cost money.

Some of these will be relationship choices, good for our
mental health and happiness, moving us out of isolation

and into community — our human rather than material environment. Under current circumstances, many people tend to relate more intensely to cars or clothes or media or electronic gadgets than they do to actual people. Gradually, we will be forced to remember that other people are actually very interesting and infinite fun (if sometimes aggravating) to engage with. Similarly we will even learn to find productive choices more intriguing than consumptive ones. Do I want to spend my time and energy making a bigger garden plot, or repairing the roof or finishing a sculpture? Despite the toxic individualism of our culture, we will even pay more attention to collective choices. Do *we* want to buy a new push lawn mower for the street's neighbors, so that we can all save on power-mower gas and get some needed exercise besides? Do *we* think candidate X really has our interests at heart, or will she or he vote as demanded by the campaign funders? Do *we* want more parking or better transit service?

In short, the balance between the individual and his or her surroundings will change in quite fundamental ways, just as it has changed (toward individualism and alienation) in the era of cheap oil. Where, in the past, we have focused on what and how to *buy*, we will have time and necessity to focus on what must be *done*. And since dwindling resources and costlier energy will put stringent premiums on efficiency, compactness, cooperation and multiple functions, we will look at a whole host of things in new ways. *Consumer Reports* might even take to saying that, after due examination, some products are simply not worth buying.

Cohousing (living in mutually designed multiple-dwelling and usually car-free mini-communities) won't be just an optional lifestyle choice among well educated, idealistic or religiously linked people; it'll be the generally accepted best way to live, especially for single parents.

Community Supported Agriculture (people "subscribing" to the produce grown on a nearby farm and delivered to their door according to the seasons) won't be something that only the dedicated do: it will be the universally best way to obtain a healthy diet cheaply — and maybe you'll also visit the farm to see where your food comes from, or to help pick it. People who no longer have private cars will turn to car-sharing in various ways, but also to jitney services run by people who still have cars and discover they can make a living by running informal taxi-type operations. Community gardens, where neighbors share plots and water and compost, working side by side or together, will be a standard feature of most neighborhoods, even in large cities — where vacant lots and rooftops can produce astonishing amounts of vegetables. The sharing of tools, especially expensive power tools, will become routine among do-it-yourselfers. Bartering stuff and trading work, age-old patterns in hard-bitten communities, will become established as features of middle-class life — not only via the Internet, but through community bulletin boards on the street.

In short, we'll see a flourishing of new ways to help each other. Necessity really *is* a reliable mother of invention. And in our individual lives, we will find many people adopting what I've called the green-triangle approach. As you look over your daily life, imagine a triangle whose points are environment, budget and health. It miraculously turns out that if you make a change aimed at improving one of those points, it will also help the others. Suppose, for example, you sell your car and acquire a workable used bicycle for your modest commute. You will cease putting auto emissions into the air. You will also save plenty of money, even if you occasionally have to rent a car or take a taxi. And you will get some healthy exercise. But green triangulation also works if you start with health. If you cut down on meat, you do your cardiovascular system a big favor. You also reduce the environmental damage caused to soil and water by live-stock production. And of course you save money. And if you start with the third point of the triangle, your budget, spending less will reduce your environmental impacts and probably improve your health. The green triangle can stim-ulate your imagination toward ways to live better with less.

The new era we've entered is not going to be easy, but then neither was most of the past. In the period after World War II, the GI bill, strong unions and American economic supremacy gave us a vastly expanded working middle class. This is now being brought to an end by the triple crisis of Peak Oil, global heating and punitive globalization, along with the effects of a long rightward slide in US political life. Most Americans are now going to be poorer and live sim-pler lives. The real question is, will our response be to get smarter — and more militant?

The Lagom Solution

by Alan AtKisson

ALAN ATKISSON is president of the AtKisson Group, an
international consultancy. He has written two books,
*Believing Cassandra: An Optimist Looks at a Pessimist's
World* (Chelsea Green, 1999) and *The ISIS Agreement:
How Sustainability Can Improve Organizational Performance and Transform the World* (Earthscan, 2008). Alan
is the originator of the ISIS Method, a step-by-step process for teaching, learning and doing sustainable development in practice, as well as the lead designer of the
ISIS Accelerator, a comprehensive set of tools designed
to support education and strategic action on sustainability. Alan continues to perform as a musician and song-
writer and has released four albums on the independent
label Rain City Records. A dual citizen of Sweden and
the United States, he lives in Stockholm with his wife and
partner Kristina AtKisson, who also works as a sustainability consultant and trainer, and their two children.

A T THE AGE OF 40, I moved to Sweden and learned
Swedish. Like any wealthy country, Sweden is full of
shopping malls and the advertisements that drive us to them.
Although once feared by US leaders as a bastion of social-
ism (President Dwight Eisenhower once gave a speech on
the topic), this Nordic country has always been a tiny capitalist powerhouse, from Alfred Nobel's string of European

dynamite and gunpowder factories in the 1800s, to today's global brands like Ikea or Hennes & Mauritz (H&M). A visiting colleague from Tunisia, who had spent time in both the US and Sweden, reflected to me that Swedes seemed to him even more obsessed with shopping than Americans — which was saying quite a lot.

But despite the usual consumerist excesses that one can find here (mostly in the major cities), Sweden also has something that many other countries do not have: the concept of *lagom*.

The word *lagom*, which has no direct equivalent in English, appears often in Swedish conversation. For many people here, it captures something essential about Swedish culture as well. *Lagom* has to do with quantity, with the "how muchness" of something. *Lagom* is neither too much nor too little; but neither is it just "enough." (There is different word for that.) Meaning "exactly the right amount," it can be applied to anything: stuff, people, the size of a room, the food on your plate…even the atmosphere at a party. If it were a place, it would lie somewhere north of sufficiency, but south of excess. It is hard to say exactly how much it is, but you know it when you experience it. When something is "just right," it is *lagom*.

I originally encountered *lagom* when I first visited my wife, who is Swedish, in her apartment outside of Stockholm. The Swedish style of simple-but-comfortable home furnishings has always appealed to me. But I was amazed to learn that she owned only two towels. (Actually, it turned out that she owned three, but the third she used only for travel. Swedes tend to bring their own towels.) Coming from America, where most people have an entire closet devoted to a mountain of towels, the concept of owning just two towels was mind-boggling. How did she do it?

"When the bathroom towels are dirty, I wash them.

When they wear out, I buy two more — and very good ones, so they last a long time."

"Why do I need more than two?" she asked. "*Det är lagom.*"

The word *lagom* is pronounced, like so much of Swedish, melodically. The "la" is a falling tone. The "gom" (rhymes with "home" in American English) is a shorter syllable that starts right back up at the same tone where the "la" started. Swedish is something like Chinese; if you don't *sing* the word right, you probably won't be understood.

Understanding *lagom* will help you understand why Scandinavian design tends to look minimalist. Materials should not be wasted. Function precedes form. Nothing is gained by excess; and very likely, something important is lost.

The general belief about the origins of *lagom* dates back to the Viking era. When a bowl of beer was passed around the circle, it was expected that everyone would drink exactly the right amount for them…and leave exactly the right amount for everyone else as well. *Lagom* is two words together, *lag* ("team") and *om* ("around"). Embedded in the concept is a sense of togetherness, or "social solidarity." Indeed, social solidarity is another concept that is far more prevalent in Swedish life; a commitment to the well-being of others, and not just oneself, is at the core of both the culture and the political system. One of the harshest critiques I have heard uttered against a person, for example, is that she or he is not sufficiently *solidarisk* — an adjective for which I can find no equivalent in English either.

In contrast, when it comes to thinking about responses to overconsumption and consumerism, we English-speakers are stuck with an inadequate vocabulary. "Enough" sounds to most of our ears as though it had the word "barely" just in front of it. For some reason, "enough" never sounds like…

enough. Other words used commonly in talking about the issues of overconsumption do not fare much better. "Balance" sounds difficult; one eventually loses it. "Sufficiency" carries the whiff of technical economic jargon, and has even more of that "barely" feeling in it. Even "Simplicity," despite its ups and downs in marketing and magazine circles, tends to appeal largely to folks with either a strong sense of moral commitment or a serious case of overwhelm.

The world needs better concepts for thinking about how much, in terms of stuff and consumption, is the right amount — and the Swedes have given us a word for it. The concept of *lagom* can be applied to everything from cake to carbon dioxide emissions. What is *lagom* for chocolate cake? For me, it's usually a bit more than "enough." But what's *lagom* for CO_2? Only as much as the ecological systems of the Earth can reabsorb, and no more. *Lagom* allows for more than enough — but it still sets limits.

In looking around the world and talking to people about *lagom*, I have so far found only one other culture that has an equivalent: there is a Japanese phrase that means "I have just what I need." In fact, I am told that there is more than just a phrase for this idea: there is even a god. Apparently, in Japan one can leave offerings at the temple of the god of having exactly what you need.

What if our economic aspirations were organized not around the concept of "growth," but around the concept of having exactly what you need — *lagom*? Not that all of Sweden is organized that way; although my wife is hardly an extremist, she is a more enthusiastic *lagom*-ist than many of her fellow Swedes. There are plenty of cases of modern-day "affluenza" here, including a creeping incursion by SUVs on the roads. And Sweden does have a history of occasionally taking a bit more than it needs. (Imagine the Vikings taking only *lagom* when they plundered!)

So I have begun an attempt both to export this word and to celebrate it here at home in Sweden, where it can sometimes also be used ironically: it's a terrible thing, for example, to call your boyfriend *lagom*. Some people here complain about living in the "land of *lagom*," of "middle milk" that has just two percent fat; they long for a bit more excess. As the Buddhists remind us, everything should be taken in moderation, including moderation.

Lagom may be tricky for English-speakers to pronounce. But it has an attractive quality that "enough," "sufficient" and even "simple" often lack. Most people in the world do not want enough. They want more. They certainly want more than the bare minimum, and research suggests they want more than those around them. This desire for more seems to be deeply wired in the human organism. We developed over millennia in hostile environments, both natural and social. To have more than we need has always been our first defense against the vagaries of an uncertain future. Hoarding is the first act of those who believe themselves to be in the path of a storm (or a marauding army of plundering Vikings, for that matter).

So while there will always be those of us who love the idea of "enough-ness" and "Voluntary Simplicity," it seems likely that such concepts may never quite be…well… *enough* to transform the masses of humanity. Nor are they likely to transform the marauding army of global corporations vying to fill our houses with stuff, in a kind of reverse-Viking-plunder operation.

But it does seem possible to promote a sensible Swedish sense of *lagom* worldwide — and to find other good words for it — because it speaks more to what people actually want. Let's admit that it is very nice to have good shoes. No one can be faulted for wanting them. But does a person really need 15 pairs? No. But is one pair enough? Perhaps not.

Lagom acknowledges that people have varying needs and desires at different times. They want nice things, and comfort, and security. They want more than the bare minimum, and they might even need it. If their desire for more than enough is accepted, even supported, perhaps they would be more willing to consider how much is too much.

Clearly, in those parts of the world obsessed with acquisition (including Sweden), and curiously unconcerned about the disappearance of polar ice and polar bears, we are far beyond the limits of *lagom*. Once, I took my wife to visit a Sam's Club in the US. As most people reading this will know, these are huge retail warehouse stores full of consumer goods, on sale cheap. The buildings are large enough to house a submarine assembly plant. You can buy everything from taco shells to trampolines to model wooden boats, by the crate. The shopping carts are as big as a small car (no, you can't buy cars, not yet). Walking around the aisles of one of these stores has always brought forth several radically different feelings in me: raw consumer lust, great moral outrage and aching environmental angst.

But my wife's response, when she first encountered one of these places, was more practical: "I suppose people can save quite a lot of money here. And it's better to buy some things in larger quantities. (Not towels.) But perhaps it's just very tempting to take too much in such a place."

Nobody really needs too much, and in fact, most people don't really want it. But nobody wants too little. Perhaps our vision for a sustainable world should include not just enough for all, but *lagom* for all, with fewer temptations to take too much.

And while I could write a lot more about this proposed new addition to the world's vocabulary, perhaps this essay, too, is now *lagom*.

[Author's note: An earlier version of this essay, entitled "The Right Amount," was originally published in *The Simple Living Newsletter*, January 2001, and several other publications. It has been updated and adapted for this book.]

Creating a Life You Love

by Wanda Muszynski

WANDA MUSZYNSKI, whose Polish parents immigrated to Canada as refugees following World War II, earned degrees at the University of Alberta and Concordia University in Montreal (Commerce and Business Administration). Fluently trilingual (English, Polish and French), Wanda spent the greater part of her professional life working in Canada in the field of advertising, specifically, media planning.

In 2002, Wanda joined the staff of Komozja S. A. in Czestochowa, Poland, a family-owned business with 200 employees making handcrafted blown-glass Christmas ornaments. Wanda is a founding member of the Canadian Foundation for Polish Studies (CFPS), whose objective is to foster an awareness of Polish history, culture and issues within mainstream Canadian educational, community and media institutions.

I ONCE WORKED for an advertising agency whose slogan was "WE GET THERE FIRST!" The phrase was embedded into the footer of our PowerPoint presentations. It found its way onto our corporate T-shirts, our company letterhead and our coffee cups. Getting there first, it seemed, carried a lot of weight in business — the *first* to innovate, the *first* to set new industry standards, the *first* to put a man on the moon, etc.

Staring at this slogan, I remember thinking, why does it have to be a race? And where, exactly, is *there*? I knew these were heretical thoughts in the mind of an otherwise loyal company executive, but for me, they were yet another signal that my work life was sliding out of sync with my values.

Don't get me wrong. I am a *big* believer in the private enterprise system — a system that creates economic opportunity for its citizens and rewards initiative. I am grateful to have been born and raised in a country (Canada) that subscribes to this system. And, while I know how easy it is to take pot shots at big business, I have to say that over the course of my many years of working with marketing departments, I met a lot of good people who cared about more than just making a buck — many of whom did not hesitate to lend their skills (fundraising, managing, organizing) to any number of worthy causes.

My own move toward simplifying my life was propelled by a need to spend my time doing work that was more meaningful to me. The itch to change something permanently and for the better became strongest in the mid-1990s. I was 14 years into my career and 10 years into my marriage. My husband was in a managerial position similar to mine at another advertising agency. I felt that we had the kind of insights into one another's worlds that would permanently inoculate us against any type of marital crises. It turned out that I was wrong.

Maybe it was because both of us were running so hard and so fast that we raced right past each other. We did what I suppose many other couples do all the time: take each other utterly and completely for granted. My husband and I had also been trying, unsuccessfully, for years to start a family. As it slowly dawned on us that our dream life might never materialize, we started to dream different dreams. Separate dreams led to separate vacations, separate interests and, eventually, to separate lives.

It was on one of those separate vacations that the seed of a new life started to sprout in my brain. I took a trip to Poland, the birthplace of my parents. I didn't want to be just another tourist, so I signed on for a summer language course. Our family had no relatives left in Poland. My parents had lived in the eastern part of the country that was invaded by the Soviet Union at the outbreak of the World War II in 1939. My mother was not quite ten years old when Soviet soldiers marched into her town, forcibly entered people's homes and told them that they had an hour to pack and report to the train station. Mostly women, children and the elderly — since younger men had already been rounded up and imprisoned — they, along with tens of thousands of other Polish families from surrounding villages, were being deported to slave labor camps in Siberia. They had no idea where they were going or for how long. My father's story was similar.

My parents were among the lucky few who eventually made it out of the Soviet Gulag. At the war's end, their respective families immigrated to Canada. That's where my parents met and where I and my siblings were born and raised. I grew up listening to my parents' language, but I couldn't speak it. I knew that they loved their new country, Canada. To them, there truly was no better place in the world to live and raise a family. At the same time, I could sense a longing for the world, the culture, the home they were taken away from. I wanted to know more about that world, and I wanted to become competent enough in the language to interact with the people.

I picked a small resort town near the Baltic Sea for my summer course (my plan was to spend the mornings in class and the afternoons on the white, sandy beaches of the Baltic). It was 1996, and Poland was still shaking off the heavy yoke of communism. Many of the buildings were drab and gray on the outside, but inside I frequently discovered another world: one of vibrant, colorful clubs and restaurants usually set up by young people who had long dreamed of restoring their homeland to its European past. I started to think of these places as Poland's best-kept secret: restaurant interiors that looked like something out of Tuscany, Irish pubs, American jazz bands. It was clear to me that, despite its half century under the communist boot, this country was full of closet capitalists. Now, for the first time, they were able to indulge their entrepreneurial imaginations in a way that we, Canadians and Americans, had taken for granted our entire lives. What added to the excitement for me was that at no other time in history had there been a model of a society transitioning from a communist system to a capitalist one. It was the Wild East. Rules were getting invented on the spot. People were constantly asking me about how things worked in "my world" — they just assumed that if you were from "the West," you knew. That atmosphere of mid-1990s Poland in social and economic transition was exhilarating. I wanted to be part of it.

When I returned to Montreal, I had a heart-to-heart with my boss. I told her that I needed to reinvent myself and that I wanted to do it in Poland. I talked about my need to become part of something bigger — a pioneer in a society that was struggling to find its way in a dramatic new reality.

My boss's response (and for this, I will always be grateful): "If I can't talk you into staying, then I'll help you get to where you want to go." And she did.

Two years later, with her help, I had secured an ad agency position in Warsaw. While I knew that my days in that industry were numbered, it made sense to start by doing the work I knew how to do (you do the job you *have* to do till you find the job you *want* to do). Taking two years to prepare for this move was *my* choice — Warsaw was ready to take me immediately, but I needed the time to wind things down. The list was long: sell the house or find responsible tenants (fortunately, my soon-to-be ex was onside), split up our belongings, throw out want you don't want, sell what you can, find storage space for what you'd like to keep. This exercise goes a long way toward curing oneself of the propensity to accumulate more. I recommend it to everyone.

Warsaw turned out to be a springboard to a whole other life. I had not been in Poland long when, through a friend, I was invited to meet a family that owned a factory making mouth-blown, hand-painted glass Christmas ornaments. Two brothers and two sisters (of my generation) had resuscitated a glassworks business started up by their parents before the communists expropriated it half a century before. I was impressed by their talent, their ingenuity, their creativity and most of all their determination.

Here and now, in a new system where people could at long last come up for air, were four entrepreneurial individuals determined to carry on their parents' tradition and recreate their success. They had the skilled glassblowers, the designers and the craftsmen, but they needed someone to handle communications between the factory and their US-based clients. I convinced them to hire me. Financially, I was taking a risk. The competitive landscape was now global and changing dramatically. China was emerging as the-factory-of-the-world, and I knew that European exporters would be in for a long, hard struggle. I'd be lucky to make half the salary that I had been pulling at the ad agency job. I also realized that the money really didn't mean that much to me. I had enough; so I made the leap.

For the last six years now, I've been working in a small town in southern Poland. It hasn't always been easy, but it has been every bit the adventure that I expected it to be. I live in a bed-and-breakfast-style hotel across the street from the factory. I have a comfortable room with a full bath. Every now and then, the hotel owners ask me if I'd like to upgrade to a suite with two rooms. I always say no. More rooms mean more stuff, and I don't want more stuff. I love the feeling of being free and unencumbered.

My uncluttered life has freed me up for many things. Old friendships have been rekindled. Travel is made easy. The friendships and the travel go together. We meet in places we want to see — Krakow, Prague, Tunis, Istanbul — but the main purpose is to just *be* with one another. It is a wonderful thing to build up a store of experiences with good friends and know that we will reminisce over them in years to come.

Travel has truly become one of my greatest passions and one of those indulgences that I permit myself several times a year. For me, transporting myself to a different world, a different culture, brings home to me the importance of the here and now — living in the moment. I don't even take photographs. I want to feel that I am truly *in* the moment and not just recording it.

When I first moved to Europe, I also promised myself that I would do my utmost to see all that I could see — simply, affordably — and that I would *not* wither away my weekends inside hermetically sealed buildings putting in the long hours I used to at the ad agency (a culture that treated chronic workaholism as a virtue). Certainly, even with Europe's network of cheap airlines, my penchant for sightseeing costs a little, but then, I don't own a car — haven't for almost ten years. I'm not the least bit fussed by taking public transportation year-round when I know it will allow me yet another trip. These are the trade-offs I'm comfortable with. The best part: I have not once, in six years, cancelled or postponed a trip because of something pressing back at the office, and nor would anyone expect me to.

I still work hard, but it's a different kind of work. I am not a cog in an impersonal machine. More like part of a family that creates jobs and struggles to meet the payroll but also maintains a very human approach to things. Owners and employees alike know that they are in this enterprise to-gether, that their success is a benefit to all and that everyone has an important role to play: artists, glass-blowers, decora-tors, marketing, shipping; we are all interdependent.

When people ask me what is the single-biggest differ-ence between my life then and my life now, it's a feeling of things finally being back in sync. Aligned. I no longer dream of escaping to a better life. This *is* a good life. It will still change, evolve in different and surprising ways, but the restlessness is gone. It may seem simplistic to say, but liv-ing life in accordance with one's values *is* a deeply satisfying thing. Problems still arise. Threats still loom on the horizon. I still have stress, but the stress is about the *right* things.

Everyday brings a number of daunting challenges, but they are so much easier to face with a group of people I care about and who share a sense of common purpose. In this tiny microcosm of a factory, I feel that my contribution and my example matter a lot. I feel that, collectively, our small successes provide...well, something of a model for other budding, home-grown entrepreneurs — people who maybe need a little boost in self-confidence to start the process of building something from nothing; people who need to break away from old dependencies on a system that came crashing down along with the Berlin Wall only two short decades ago; or people who simply need to discover that with a little effort they can take charge of their destinies.

I also feel more — what's the word? — *integrated* as a person. My Canadian self, my Polish self, my pragmatic business self, my silly off-duty self, my spiritual self are all wrapped into one. There is no need to compartmentalize (different selves for different audiences). I no longer feel that I am playing a role or that I have to censor my thoughts (sad to say, this was a basic survival skill in my old corporate life).

My simple pleasures include waking up on Saturday morning and delighting in the fact that I have no plans. I might go off to the market square, pick up my favorite English-language newspaper and spend three hours reading at an outdoor café. I might get together with some students who meet up with me every now and then just to practise their English. I might hop on a train and pay a visit to one of my favorite cities or go to one I've never seen before (I absolutely love that about living in Europe). Or, I might even decide that I'll go into the office for a few hours where I can open up a huge skylight, breathe in the fresh air and hear the birds chirping while I putter away at my desk. Either way, I feel that *I* am in control of the agenda and not the other way around.

Some of my best moments, though, come from visiting my folks back in Canada and sharing with them the day-to-day goings-on in the country from which they were once exiled (they have since visited, but it's not the same as living there). Funny, but they have never once asked me *why* I left the high-salary job and opted for this simpler life. I'm certain that they stumbled upon the answers long before I ever did. We talk about politics, people, popular shows on TV, all sorts of stuff. I can see that it leaves them with a sense of comfort — a feeling that, in the end, things turned out pretty well in their old homeland after all. As I share my stories with my parents, I can't shake off the image of their having to leave behind all of their material possessions, endure incredible hardship and come out of the experience thinking of themselves as the lucky ones. Their lives have been a lesson to me. Could that have something to do with my own life choices?

Maybe. Or, maybe not. Maybe getting to this stage is simply a function of happenstance and maturity. Either way, I'm glad to have made it...this far.

Taking Back Family Life from Overscheduling

by William J. Doherty

WILLIAM J. DOHERTY, PhD, is professor of family social science and director of the Citizen Professional Center at the University of Minnesota. A family therapist and community organizer with families, he first became involved with the idea of Simplicity through his work with parents around the cultural pressures to do too much, spend too much and over-organize the lives of children. He wrote *The Intentional Family*.

R EMEMBER THE POPULAR 1980's song, "Don't Worry, Be Happy"? Now the anthem could well be "Don't Worry, Be Busy." Never in human history have children and families have been so overscheduled. Not only are adults busier with their work lives, but family life today, as never before, revolves around children's activities such as soccer, hockey, scouts, baseball, football, piano, crafts clubs, special language classes, dance, violin, band and religious youth groups. Parents have become part-time chauffeurs and full-time recreation directors on the family cruise ship.

We know that involvement in outside activities is good for kids. But many parents and professional groups such as the American Academy of Pediatrics worry that today's frantic pace is depriving children of their time to be children, families of their time to be families and couples of their time to be married. From studies of families' time use, we are getting a picture of the problem. Compared to during the late 1970s, today's children play less, make up their own activities less often, engage in supervised sports a lot more often, spend a whole lot more time watching passively from the sidelines, have fewer unhurried conversations with their parents, have fewer family dinners each week and have fewer family vacations. These changes run deep and broad in the American population, cutting across income and ethnic groups. And they came upon us with hardly anyone paying attention.

Both common sense and research tell us that there is something wrong here. Once their children reach school age, many parents feel burdened by crammed schedules and feel a loss of family connections. Teachers talk about a generation of students weary from schedules that most adults could not handle. Research studies have shown the importance of family meals and the negative effects of skipping them. And the kids themselves are speaking up, when we listen to them. A YMCA poll of teenagers found that "not having enough time with parents" was their top concern. And a local nine-year-old boy asked his parents, for a birthday present, for more time to hang out at home.

Many reasons lie behind this problem of overscheduled kids and under-connected families. Here's a partial list I've gathered from parents across the country: more opportunities for children, more intense sports activities, more working parents, parental guilt about not doing enough for their children, safety concerns about neighborhood play, fear that one's child will miss out or be left behind and pressure for children to achieve success in many domains. An overarching explanation is that the competitive, market-oriented adult culture has invaded the family over the past two decades. We are now a nation of bigger-better-faster in almost all domains of life, including child rearing and family life.

As explained in my book *Take Back Your Kids: Confident Parenting in Turbulent Times*, the consumer culture of parenting means that well-intentioned parents see themselves as providers of services and opportunities to their children in the marketplace of child rearing. Children are seen as bundles of potential talents to be developed. Childhood has become a race for success, led by anxious parents looking around to see if their kids are keeping pace with the competition. It's exhausting, and family connections are fraying. And it's become a worldwide problem among middle-class parents. In countries like Singapore and Korea, it takes the form of intense academic competition beginning in preschool, with parents worrying that their three-year-olds are already behind. Back in the US, some New York City parents hire tutors for their two-year-olds to pass the test to get into elite preschools, which are assumed to be the ticket to Harvard — and then to a competitively successful life.

As the pace of childhood quickens for many, it has stagnated for some low-income children who lack enrichment opportunities. We're creating a two-tiered system of childhood: the frantic over-enriched child on the one hand and the under-involved and under-stimulated child on the other. Because the middle class tends to set the cultural bar, when low-income parents rise out of poverty they see their job as getting their children into traveling soccer teams instead of having dinners at home. There's a problem here: Research shows that family meals are the single most important activity to promote the academic and psychological well-being of children — family meals. If you want to give your kids opportunities, break bread with them every day.

How do we turn the tide? It starts from understanding

that we humans are pack animals, social creatures if you will. We raise our young in packs we call neighborhoods, schools and communities. Nowadays, the parent leaders of the pack are those who, with good intentions, over-schedule outside activities and under-schedule family rituals such as dinners, bedtime talks, weekend outings, visits to grandparents and just time to hang out together. They boast about how busy their families are and how well their children compete. (Have you read holiday letters recently?) They rarely talk about playing family games at home, about how close their children are to their grandparents or about leisurely family brunches on the weekend. They push local programs and facilities to offer more opportunities, to win more often and to schedule more intensely. They drive schools to give more homework to young children, despite the lack of research evidence that homework prior to middle school contributes to children's learning.

The rest of us are influenced by these parent leaders and by the song they sing in our communities. Most are good people trying to do the best for the children in today's turbo-charged, competitive culture. We have let them become leaders of the pack because the rest of us have abdicated to them. It's time, for the sake of our children and our families, for a change in leadership.

In Minnesota and other places around the country, parents have been organizing to take back their families. Balance For Success in Dakota Country, Minnesota, began by organizing a Sunday boycott of youth sports, which got the attention of the sports leaders. Now this grassroots citizen parent group is organizing community forums to bring together people on both sides of the youth sports debate. Putting Family First in Wayzata, Minnesota, is another citizens group of parents trying to influence the cultural conversation about the balance between family life and outside activities, and offering support to one another in making personal changes. In local conversations and on their websites, Putting Family First and Balance For Success are capturing families' stories of struggles, strategies and successes in taking back their life together.

Organizing works. When parents begin making changes and talking to friends and neighbors about it, they find their influence spreading across neighborhoods and faith communities. Other frantic parents gain confidence that they were not risking their children's future by saying no to certain activities, but rather that they were doing the best for their children. They start talking about having more family meals, and about taking one day a week with no scheduled activities. Parents in one private school supported a new plan to abolish advanced placement courses because they were driving a culture of frantically seeking competitive advantage for college instead of focusing on genuine learning and balanced living.

Cultural change often begins by naming a problem that has had no name, thereby challenging what the cultural common sense sees as natural and inevitable. In 1999, the citizen parents I worked with in Putting Family First named the problem of "overscheduled kids," and the cultural conversation has been building for a decade. More people are seeing the overscheduled family as an unhealthy distortion ushered in by the turbo-charged consumer culture. Objective signs suggest that the tide is turning — polls indicate a gradual return to the family dinner hour. Just as important, we are seeing the rise of a new generation of leaders of the pack, parents who proclaim balance as a family value for the 21st century.

Why I Farm

by Bryan Welch

BRYAN WELCH went to work caring for a neighbor's dairy goats in Anapra, New Mexico, when he was nine years old. The connection he formed with the animals and the desert where they browsed helped secure his lifelong bond with the natural world. Bryan's father, his grandfathers and his great-grandfathers all grew up as ranchers, farmers and drovers, their lives intimately linked to land and livestock.

In 1996, Bryan helped form Ogden Publications, the company he still runs that today owns *Mother Earth News*, *Utne Reader*, *Natural Home* and a number of other magazines and websites dedicated to sustainable lifestyles, rural lifestyles and Simplicity. His blog is called Rancho Cappuccino, in honor of the farm where he and his wife Carolyn raise organic, grass-fed cattle, sheep, goats and chickens.

I WRITE THIS during the most bittersweet of our seasons, late fall or early winter depending on the mood and the weather. Tomorrow it might be 20 degrees and driving sleet, or it might be 70 and sunny.

It's the time of year when we kill the animals — the cattle, sheep and goats — we will eat next year. Just a few months ago, they were the spirits of spring, filling the pastures with the joyful, bouncing exuberance of new life. In a few weeks, their meat will be in my freezers, and those of my friends', on our tables and, quite literally, part of us.

We raise most of our own food and earn a little income from our small Kansas farm. But in our hearts, it's more art than business. We draw a frame around our 50 acres of prairie. Nature fills it with color and motion. Every day brings new pigments, new images and new performances.

Some farmers I know seem never to consider their animals as anything other than livestock — literally their stock in trade. To farmers like us they are partners, friends, entertainers and something close to family.

People often ask, "How can you eat your own animals?" Sometimes it's a sincere question, meant to explore the emotions associated with raising sentient beings for meat. Often I think it's more of an accusation: "How can you be so callous?"

Sometimes I think to myself, "How can you be so thoughtless as to eat animals without knowing them? Without knowing how they lived? Without making sure they were treated kindly and with respect?"

My father, both my grandfathers and all my great-grandparents were grass farmers. By that I mean that their vocation was to raise or find forage to sustain the livestock that was their livelihood. It's quite possible that every generation of my family since prehistoric times has followed a herd of grazing animals — either domesticated or wild — through its lifetime and down its nomadic path across the ages. We have always been in direct contact and in a kind of kinship with the animals that end up on our table. I believe it's a "natural" relationship in the deepest and most profound sense of that word.

I don't mean to suggest that everyone should raise their own meat. But it's perverse, isn't it, that people in our society seem to consider it more civilized to eat animals they don't know? Meanwhile, industrial agriculture treats meat animals as nothing more than cogs in the machine, without regard for their happiness. Very few people these days enjoy the privilege of knowing the creatures they eat, or of experiencing the miraculous transformation of their energy into our own vitality.

Vegans deserve respect. They have made a conscious sacrifice for a principle, and that's admirable. But the cultivated fields where their food is raised are biological wastelands where very, very few creatures can actually live. Our natural pastures teem with life. Every day we see rodents, ground-nesting birds, coyotes and myriad insects. If you look only at the number of creatures displaced or destroyed by a meal of soybeans versus the number of creatures who pay, in one sense or another, to provide us with a grass-fed, pasture-raised steak dinner, the steak could very well win the humanitarianism contest.

While I'm proud of the happy, healthy lives we give our animals, it doesn't prevent me from feeling a profound twinge of sadness as I look out over the animals in the pastures. It's a sadness I've gradually learned to embrace, a melancholy that embodies the transience of our individual existence and the sturdier, less ephemeral web of life that we, and our food, are a part of.

It's the sadness associated with life's astonishing richness and vitality. It's the sadness associated with mortality. It's the sadness we feel as we consider the impermanence of everything on this planet, everything mortal we hold dear. The sadness that makes life poignant and sweet.

And it gives me a profound feeling of gratitude, also.

The exercise of raising my own food forms the bedrock of my conservation ethic. I certainly care about the rainforests of Malaysia and the Amazon, but I care *for* this small piece of Kansas prairie, which in turn cares for me. My concern for the world's coral reefs and alpine tundra is informed and enhanced by my stewardship of the grasses and forbs that carpet the earth around my home. In the act of finding nourishment directly from the earth, I've developed a deeper emotional attachment with the planet as a whole.

One chilly day, I was working on a fence far out in a new pasture, and I kept smelling food. I checked my pockets for old sandwich wrappers. I checked the toolbox for snacks. I smelled the cuffs of my seldom-laundered work shirt. Then I realized I had been sitting in the wild onions that sprout green among the brown grasses all the way through the Kansas winter. They smelled like hamburgers.

Like any art form, nature rewards people who've studied its methods and its media. For the farmer, that study is part of a vocation. It's a vocation that, at its best, can deepen our appreciation of nature profoundly. The fact that we must destroy life to create life is a subject that farmers seldom discuss, but we understand the contradiction implicitly. I don't believe it's possible to fully appreciate life without that understanding.

The sheep and goats eat the green onion shoots. Sometimes I smell them on their breath. I enjoy watching the goats eating the dry seed heads off sunflowers. In late summer, they work the edges of the pastures with their heads stretched high over their backs, crunching one protein-rich nugget after another. I puzzle over the way sheep like to trim the grass down to a slick butch, like the manicured greens on a golf course, favoring the new growth next to the ground over the big standing clumps. Cattle, on the other hand, seem to enjoy a nice big mouthful.

Twenty-five years ago, I was an avid hiker and backpacker. A skier and a climber. I probably spent 45 days a year in the outdoors. I slept outside five or six nights a year. I knew I was missing a lot.

Now I'm outside every night, checking on the livestock and closing the chicken house. I see the ice crystals form a halo around the moon. I watch the sun come up nearly every day. I know what's blooming and which birds are coming through. What the soil smells like as the seasons change. How it feels to be outside on the worst night of the year watching coyotes try to open the door of the henhouse. I think I have an inkling of what it must feel like to have an empty belly on a cold night and to smell all those warm, plump hens just a few feet away. I watch a coyote trying to slip a paw under the swinging door. I consider whether I would let him take a trophy if he prevails. Probably not, but I admire his ingenuity.

I still miss a lot, but I see much more of nature than I did when I was outdoors purely for recreation. Now when I go on a fishing trip or take a long hike, I think I see nature more clearly and notice details I wouldn't have before I came to see the natural environment from the perspective of a farmer. I've appreciated more of the natural world as I've come to know it better. Somehow knowing the difference between the track of a box turtle and the track of a snapping turtle makes it a lot more interesting to look for tracks.

For me the difference between hiking and farming is the difference between listening to music and playing music. As a hiker, I enjoy the dramatic rhythms and splashy vistas of the mountains. As a farmer, I play dense, vigorous prairie music.

I get a lot of blood, and dirt and manure on my hands and my clothes these days. I get calluses and scars. I get a lot of laughs watching my animals figure out their lives, and I feel melancholy when it's time to kill them.

Yeah, I have a lot more death in my life than I did before.

And, paradoxically, that's part of the reason why I feel like I have a lot of life in my life.

That's why I farm.

Why People of Faith Must Care for the Planet

by Matthew Sleeth

MATTHEW SLEETH, MD, a former emergency room director and chief of medical staff, now writes, preaches and teaches full-time about faith and the environment. Together with his wife, Nancy, and their two children, he helps lead the growing creation care movement. He wrote *Serve God, Save the Planet: A Christian Call to Action*.

What does it profit my brethren if someone says he has faith but does not have works? Can faith save him?.... For as the body without the spirit is dead, so faith without works is also dead.

— JAMES 2:14 AND 26 NKJ

IT WAS A triple-h day in the nation's capital — hazy, hot and humid. A dome of smog hung over the city and extended far beyond the capital beltway. The weatherman told those with illnesses to stay indoors, but eight-year-old Etta and her brother went to a neighborhood playground.

I began my afternoon shift in the ER wing of the children's hospital while Etta and her brother were running through a sprinkler to cool off. As Etta exerted herself, her airways began reacting to the smog. The muscles that line the bronchioles of her airways involuntarily contracted, while the mucous cells began a pathologic overproduction of thick fluid. Within a few seconds, this fluid buildup became what we call an asthma attack.

Etta's brother ran back home for her inhaler, and bystanders called 911. Within a few minutes, a rescue unit was onsite and began treating and transporting Etta. They radioed ahead that things were not going well.

A nurse flipped on the lights in a trauma room, and we assembled there. The doctor in charge of the team called out what he wanted everyone to do. I was given the job of intubating Etta, if needed. The ambulance crew arrived. She was being "bagged," meaning that the paramedic was trying to oxygenate her with a mask over her mouth and nose and an Ambu bag that forced air into her lungs. Her thin, limp body was quickly transferred to our trauma gurney.

Etta's pulse was ominously slow, and her oxygen saturation level was barely readable. The Ambu bag was hard to compress because of the resistance in her clogged airways.

"Matthew, go ahead and intubate. Tammy, get an art [arterial] line in; I want her paralyzed too," the leader called out. I lifted Etta's small hand and held a few endotracheal tubes next to her little finger. Then I selected the one closest in diameter to her finger, a trick I'd been taught for quickly getting the correct size. I paused a second to lean down and whisper in Etta's ear, which is the only way to communicate with a patient in a crowded, noisy room.

"Etta," I whispered, "I'm Dr. Matt. I'm going to put a tube in your mouth and get you breathing right." I looked into her frightened eyes. "I'm not gonna let anything bad happen to you, sweetheart," I promised. Her left hand still rested in mine, and I thought I felt a weak squeeze.

Two images from that scene still haunt me. The first was her little finger held next to those plastic endotracheal tubes.

That hand was so small and vulnerable in my oversize palm. The second image came 30 seconds after I intubated Etta. The team leader yelled for quiet. He held his stethoscope on her chest. "Give her a breath," he ordered, and I squeezed down on the bag. Etta had on a bathing suit the color of a fluorescent green hula hoop. Pictured on its front was a happy, smiling whale blowing a spout of water into the air. Etta must have loved that bathing suit. One couldn't help but smile at the frolicking whale. Trying to lift that whale by forcing air into her lungs is my second haunting memory. Despite the rescue squad, and despite the best efforts of an entire pediatric emergency department, I broke my promise to Etta. She died of air pollution on that summer day.

A decade ago, I would have told you that our family was concerned about the environment. I would have said that we were true "conservatives," working to preserve nature. That was talk. We have progressed from talking a good talk to walking a better walk. How did we go from saying we were concerned to actually making a difference?

When God called me to this creation care ministry, I was a physician — chief of staff and head of the emergency department — at one of the nicest hospitals in America. I enjoyed my job, my colleagues, my expensive home, my fast car and my big paycheck. I have since given up every one of these things.

We now live in a house the exact size of our old garage. We use less than one-third of the fossil fuels and one-quarter of the electricity we once used. We've gone from leaving two barrels of trash by the curb each week to leaving one bag every few weeks. We no longer own a clothes dryer, garbage disposal, dishwasher or lawn mower. Our yard is planted with native wildflowers and a large vegetable garden. Half of our possessions have found new homes. We are a poster family for the downwardly mobile.

What my family and I have gained in exchange is a life richer in meaning than I could have imagined. Because of these changes, we have more time for God. Spiritual concerns have filled the void left by material ones. Owning fewer things has resulted in things no longer owning us. We have put God to the test, and we have found his Word to be true. He has poured blessings and opportunities upon us. When we stopped living a life dedicated to consumerism, our cup began to run over.

Today I am one of a growing number of evangelical Christians whom the Lord is using to witness to people about his love for them and for the natural world. The Earth was designed to sustain every generation's *needs*, not to be plundered in an attempt to meet one generation's *wants*.

As I go around preaching and teaching, people share their concerns. Many want a less hectic daily schedule; others long for meaning and purpose, and the security of a rich spiritual life. Still others know what is keeping them from a closer walk with God but cannot overcome inertia to make the necessary changes.

I spoke recently with a group of men. Each described himself as born-again, and yet one told how he could not stop himself from buying cars — cars he cannot afford. Another complained of a persistent problem with credit card debt. A third described the pain — both economic and emotional — of going through a divorce. Being born anew in the Lord is crucial, but spiritual growth must follow. Spiritual growth is a journey we must actively seek.

One area we must change is our dependence on foreign oil. Despite what many think, global warming may not be the most harmful outcome of our oil habit. When people's lives become dependent on a substance, we call that addiction. The addictive potential of a substance does not necessarily correlate to the "high" it delivers. A more accurate way to judge addictive potential is to see how willing someone is to go without the substance, or how painful life becomes when it is suddenly withdrawn.

When we are addicted to something, we tend to start denying or overlooking things. We fail to question its side effects. We are willing to lower our standards.

As a Christian and a physician, I'm interested in the moral implications of our fossil fuel dependence as well as its health effects. What does devoting so much of our lives to obtaining and delivering oil do to us as a country and as individuals? The US now sends more than $200 billion a year to distant lands in exchange for oil. That means that every man, woman and child in America is sending about $700 a year to foreign countries just to feed our oil habit. One of those recipients officially forbids religious freedom. Its constitution mandates that the Earth is flat. It declares democracy a capital crime. And this country is a major, not a minor, supplier of US oil.

Ours is not the first generation to be morally blinded by building a lifestyle based upon energy from foreign shores. Slavery was the importation of cheap energy without regard to its moral cost. States that initially forbid slave energy, such as Georgia, eventually sanctioned it out of envy of the material wealth of their neighbors.

Upon meeting Harriet Beecher Stowe, the author of *Uncle Tom's Cabin*, President Lincoln was purported to have said that it was nice to meet the woman who started the Civil War. Stowe's father was among the evangelical ministers who preached the cause of abolition. Other preachers penned eloquent pro-slavery sermons. The church, like the country, found itself split by the slavery controversy. How could church leaders come to such different conclusions while reading the same Bible? Can we draw lessons from this defining moment in our history, or are we doomed to repeat it?

The Golden Rule allows us to see the moral side of many issues, including environmental ones. Love thy neighbor as thyself — one cannot claim to be a Christian and ignore the Golden Rule. It isn't a suggestion or a guideline; it is a commandment from God. What is the connection between the Golden Rule and the environment? Isn't our choice of homes, cars and appliances just a matter of lifestyle, and therefore not a moral or spiritual matter? Does God care whether I drive an SUV, leave the TV on all night or fly around the world skiing? The Bible doesn't mention any of these things. They didn't exist in Jesus' time. Yet Jesus taught the spirit of the law, not the letter. From the spirit of the law, and from the example of his love, we can determine the morality of our actions.

When I speak in a church, I bring along a case of efficient light bulbs to give to people. I refer to the Energy Star website (energystar.gov) that urges us to consume less energy. Formed by the Environmental Protection Agency under George Bush Sr.'s administration, the Energy Star site states that if every household changed its five most used bulbs to compact fluorescent light bulbs, the country could take 21 coal-fired power plants off-line tomorrow. This would keep one trillion pounds of poisonous gases and soot out of the air we breathe and would have the same beneficial impact as taking eight million cars off the road. A decrease of soot and greenhouse gases in the air translates into people who will be spared disease and death. Some 64,000 American deaths occur annually as a result of soot in the air.

Throughout my childhood, I knew of only one schoolmate with asthma. Now on a hazy day, dozens of kids in every school reach for inhalers to aid their breathing. God did not design the air to make us short of breath. It was meant to sustain us. The Harvard School of Health looked at the impact of one power plant in Massachusetts and found that it caused 1,200 ER visits, 3,000 asthma attacks and

110 deaths annually. Nationally, the soot from power plants will precipitate more than 600,000 asthma attacks.

These are just numbers, albeit large ones. For me, those numbers boil down to Etta — one young girl who died because of our poor stewardship of God's creation. For every action that we take, every item that we purchase, we must ask ourselves, "Will this bring us closer to God?"

Because of our consumer lifestyle, we are all responsible for Etta's death. Little sacrifices — changing light bulbs or hanging laundry on the line — are the small gestures that can help us save the next little girl's life.

[Excerpted from *Serve God, Save the Planet*, Zondervan, Grand Rapids, MI, April 1, 2007.]

Nearing Enough

by Linnea Johnson

LINNEA JOHNSON writes essays, stories, poems, plays and novels, yearns for truth, aches for wisdom but usually can settle for peaches and blueberries nestled in a flaky shortbread crust. Her *Swedish Christmas* poems in performance are forthcoming as a book-and-CD duo. A collection of poems, *Augury*, will be published in 2009. Her book, *The Chicago Home*, won Alice James Books' first Beatrice Hawley Award. Linnea holds a BA, MA and PhD, has taught in colleges and universities and wishes she still did. Once she lived beside a big lake, then beside an ocean; now she lives near a seasonal pond, longing for an ocean, a big lake or the occasional lavish rain.

B Y CANDLELIGHT and snuggled away under quilts in a cozy, slant-ceiling guest room one winter's night long ago, I read Helen and Scott Nearing's *Living the Good Life*, which my host had left on the bedside table for me.

The Nearings lived a self-sufficient life in the 1930s and 1940s in rural Vermont and, later into the 1990s, in Maine, their principles directing their choices. They wrote:

> We maintain that a couple, of any age … with a minimum of health, intelligence and capital, can adapt themselves to country living, learn its crafts, overcome its difficulties, and build up a life pattern rich

in simple values and productive of personal and social good.

Through their many books, they stimulated thousands to seek satisfaction through Simplicity.

As for me, my firsthand childhood experience with farms, besides mooing back to the cows on the farms we passed on family summer vacations driving west, was visiting Chicago's ŒFarm in the Zoo, in Lincoln Park where cows walked on concrete, chickens lived indoors under lights and other creatures were out of sight and represented by a chirping, squawking soundtrack emanating from painted scenery.

I grew up in Chicago, the daughter of a musician and an emigrant, who had left his family's farm in Sweden as soon as he had sufficient borrowed kronor to serve as ship's passage to the USA. He spun many grand and gritty stories of backbreaking work farming obstinate potatoes, defiant carrots and mulish rye on the stony sand of southwestern Sweden. Apparently I missed his irony and responded almost entirely to the humor and romance of his splendid stories, because I grew up wanting to live among horses and cows and chickens, all of whom would be, for me, necessarily self-cleaning, largely self-catering and surrounded by lovely leafy greens, self-planting and self-sustaining. I didn't picture myself doing actual work — nothing that would get me dirty, anyway.

Of course, I would slaughter neither pink piggies nor storied veggies nor warm lowing cattle; I couldn't imagine eating anything I lived among, knew or grew. I'd live on love, ideals and ideas. I would be there not to muck out stalls or tug up vegetables root-tethered to stones, but I'd be there to pet and to sing nature, and to write ditties and little stories about everything ruffled and thriving.

Nonetheless, inside of me simmered nascent variations on the themes of the Nearings' initial questions, dilemmas and fears — those bubbling questionings shared by anyone who desires to live a simpler, less routinized, more socially sensible life, with sun, wind and rain on their faces and organic food in their bellies, while perhaps leaving behind them high-rises and fluorescent lights, suburbs and office cubbies, processed air and food and water, the proverbial Joneses and those ubiquitous racing rats equipped with nettlesome cellphones and pesky beepers. What to do? How to do it? Where? Alone? Coupled? In community? Many of us long to design a life freed from material clutter, time and energy waste and nonessentials, to feel as the Nearings felt, "as free as a caged wild bird who finds himself once more on the wing."

Discovering Helen and Scott Nearing that night sparked me to articulate many free-floating, amorphous, unspoken questions. I learned that Helen Knothe's (1904–1995) curiosity, early study of music, Eastern religion and theosophy led her to India, and then to Australia to live in community on Sydney Harbor. She said of meeting Scott in 1930, "There started my real-life education." Like me, she was a searcher, always questioning. I was intrigued.

Then there was Scott Nearing (1883–1983), well educated and teaching in higher education. He wrote textbooks, pamphlets and essays and lectured widely, protesting inequity, exploitation and social injustice as his way of life, as a tenet of living. In *Conscience of a Radical* (1965), he wrote, "My studies and my personal experiences led me to avoid superficial living; led me to dig to the roots of personal life and social problems; led me, in other words, to become a radical."

In 1919, Scott was tried by a US federal grand jury (and cleared) on charges of obstructing recruitment and enlistment in the US military. He had written a pamphlet, *The Great Madness*, asserting that the causes of World War I were largely commercial, benefiting corporations and the wealthy.

Scott Nearing criticized unjustness and hypocrisy wherever he found it and was ousted from the Communist Party for having published a book which the Party heartily disliked. Scott was a union organizer in the 1930s, like my dad who protested Republic Steel's draconian attempts to keep workers from unionizing, and who saw goons gun down companions on either side of him. As a family, we never once crossed a picket line, a tradition I keep.

By 1930, Scott Nearing had lost a succession of four academic jobs because of his radical views on a matrix of issues such as opposing child labor and opposing US military imperialism. Like Scott Nearing, I had, now and then, taken unjust laws to the point of confetti and worse/better — protesting the nullification of civil rights for people of color, lesbians and gays, demonstrating and working against the presence of the Viet Nam War in American life and actively working to enable women to make our own reproductive choices. I wrote gadfly essays against capitalism and imperialism, organized and watched fizzle a number of unionizing attempts, and I was forced to lose a much-loved and successful college teaching career because I was an outspoken feminist and lesbian.

Kinship. I felt kinship here. Thoroughgoing kinship.

Together Helen and Scott moved to New York City, where they "were exceedingly poor" and yet were "convinced that life could be good and were determined to make ours so." From the beginning, the Nearings made the decision to leave the "wage slavery" of a market economy and, instead, to commit to a "use economy." They wrote that "a market economy seeks by ballyhoo to bamboozle consumers into buying things they neither need nor want, thus compelling them to sell their labor power as a means of paying for their purchases."

"Homesteading," Scott Nearing wrote in *The Making of a Radical*, "is based on the production of goods and services which are [used] directly without the intervention of the market. In our case we raised food and ate it, cut fuel and burned it, constructed buildings and lived in them, thus eliminating the major cash costs of living.

They developed a ten-year "pay-as-you-go" plan, their "Constitution of...household organization" for living wisely and for avoiding debt:

> [To] make a living under conditions that would preserve and enlarge joy in workmanship, would give a sense of achievement, thereby promoting integrity and self-respect; would assure a large measure of self-sufficiency and thus make it more difficult for civilization to impose restrictive and coercive economic pressures, and make it easier to guarantee the solvency of the enterprise.
>
> One of the chief factors that took us out of the city into the country was an awareness of the menace to health arising out of food processing and poisoning and a determination to safeguard ourselves against it.... Food processing, poisoning, and drugging is undermining the health of the American people as well as yielding large profits to the individuals and corporations engaged in processing, poisoning and drugging.
>
> Commodity production and high-pressure selling have turned millions of talented humans into spectators who stand outside all the creative processes of nature and society and feel their own creative impulses shrivel and die.... Following the rhythms of

nature provides more than a formal education; it stimulates an unfolding and growth and attaches the fortunate individual irrevocably to Mother Earth.

The Nearings were committed to raising as much food as they could, given local soil and climate, and to eating with the seasons. They would keep no animals; they were vegetarians who ate raw whole food. This, in turn, meant that they spent scant time in food preparation.

In *The Good Life Album of Helen and Scott Nearing*, a photographic memoir, Helen Nearing wrote:

> Born and brought up in the richest nation on earth, with its multitudinous gadgets and gimcracks as part and parcel of our daily lives, we realized that we must be prepared to reject these toys, to strike out for ourselves and to pioneer in the real sense of that term.

Helen and Scott Nearing designed a life free from consumerism, but they had zero desire to drop out of society. In *The Good Life Album of Helen and Scott Nearing*, they wrote:

> We were not seeking to escape. Quite the contrary, we wanted to find a way in which we could put more into life and get more out of it. We were not shirking obligations but looking for an opportunity to take on more worthwhile responsibilities. The chance to help, improve, and rebuild was more than an opportunity. As citizens, we regarded it as an assignment.

The Nearings chose to stay in the United States over becoming expatriates, and chose New England for its seasons and its old-world lineage. In Vermont, in 1932, they bought a rundown 65-acre farm nestled in a lovely wilderness setting. "Conveniences," they wrote, "consisted of a pump and a black iron sink in the kitchen and a shovel-out back-house at one end of the woodshed."

In *Living the Good Life*, they asserted, "We were seeking an affirmation, a way of conducting ourselves among those values which we considered essential to the good life… values including: Simplicity, freedom from anxiety or tension, an opportunity to be useful and to live harmoniously." They generated community by lecturing and writing and by hosting visitors to their homestead. They also sold at cost or gave away parcels of their land to like-minded people who then designed their own versions of the good life.

That candlelit night long ago, I read about how Scott and Helen developed their Good Life Formula, built their first stone house while gardening among Vermont boulders, and about their deciding upon raising cash crops to round out their livelihood.

When Vermont began to be gobbled up by paper companies and the ski industry, the Nearings moved, writing: "Why not spend the next…years beside the sea?" In the spring of 1952, Helen, 49, and Scott, 70, moved to Cape Rosier, Maine, which then was still isolated and affordable.

The Good Life is an integrated balance of all work necessary to a thoroughgoing, unequivocal, absolute life, including embracing friends, developing live soil, being socially aware and useful, growing vital food and creating leisure time, music, writing and art. Their Good Life strategy also includes using available building materials and doing the work of putting up one's own stone and wood buildings, and even making many pieces of equipment; the Nearings fashioned ladders and sleds, limiting the need to purchase much of their equipment. If they needed a bulldozer, chainsaw, plow or tractor for a few hours or days, they would rent, trade or barter for them with their neighbors.

Helen Nearing wrote: "We made serious and various attempts to live at five levels: with nature; by doing our daily stint of bread labor; by carrying on our professional activities; by constant association with our fellow citizens; and by unremitting efforts to cultivate the life of the mind and spirit." These five levels of living were contained in what they came to call their "four-four-four formula." Four hours of each day were directed toward "bread labor," the work that grows food or shovels out the outhouse. Four hours a day were devoted to "professional activity," according to one's skills, loves and special competencies, whether that be playing the violin or writing books. Four hours a day were "dedicated to fulfilling our obligations and responsibilities as members of the human race and as participants in various local, regional, national and world civic activities."

For me, reading the lived principles of the Nearings was a watershed event, a call to a pioneering occasion of my own. My "pioneering" began in sorting through the received ethics of my childhood as well as kicking the tires of the values I'd modified or developed in early adulthood.

By exploring the Nearing's Good Life principles, I felt free for the first time to discard commands that were supposedly zinged from the heavens by some Ozzie Wizard or by a retribution-filled, lightning-slinging deity. The Nearings didn't say that not raising one's own food consigned you to an everlasting furnace and to subsist on an eternal diet of seething bowls of brimstone. No, they said, indemnify yourself from being slaves of a market you do not and cannot control. And, oh, by the way, bite into this juicy, healthy and healthful, crunchy apple!

In meeting the minds of the Nearings, I learned that one did not have to choose between a life of being ground to dust by backbreaking farming or by a life filled only with thinking, writing and acting. The Nearings' principles of simple living, as I read and continue to read them, show us how to recognize and make time for the life of the mind, for music, for reading and writing and for civic engagement, all of which are important to me. Elated by the Nearings' writings, more than once I have picked myself up, dusted myself off and assembled my gang of principles free of the brambles and thorns and poison and scalpels of Holy and Moral and Only and Should, and I have found friends and developed strategies for living that suit me and are consistent with and challenging to the joyous, angry, interested person I am.

Indeed, my array of principles work together as a kind of a dowsing rod, helping me find answers and questions and work necessary and refreshing as clean spring water. Like the Nearings, I continually ask myself: Can we feed ourselves from our own gardens? Is a principled life really a possibility in today's world? Can I learn all I need to know? How best can I integrate the life of the mind and continue to do my art/music/writing even as I pick off chewing creatures from my Swiss chard? Can I really live what I believe?

The Nearings asserted that capitalist culture irritates the hunting-and-gathering instinct beyond need, beyond wanting, even beyond longing and, indeed, to addiction, and to greed. Perhaps the corrective is to, like the Nearings, move away from induced neediness toward the sanity of satiety. That is, to move away from the peripatetic search for "More" toward "Enough."

The Nearings' legacy continues to be the polestar, gyroscope, strategy map, heart, conscience and plumb line for living a good life, a simple life, a principled life — simple as a perfectly balanced Shaker chair, for example, or simple as my rather good, cheery cherry pie. So, stop by some time and let's talk principles, Simplicity and passion...with some pie.

Culture as a Guidepost
for a Balanced Life

by Cathy O'Keefe

CATHY O'KEEFE teaches recreation and leisure studies at the University of South Alabama in Mobile. She and her husband, Dennis, raised five children and belong to a community called L'Arche, formed around persons with developmental disabilities. She is particularly committed to working with people who are actively dying, making videos with them for their families. Cathy is attracted to the Simplicity movement as a means of freeing up time in order to spend it enjoyably with family and friends. The writings of St. Francis of Assisi and other religious figures who chose to live simply have been meaningful to her.

To know what you prefer, instead of humbly saying Amen to what the world tells you you ought to prefer, is to have kept your soul alive.

— ROBERT LOUIS STEVENSON

ONE OF THE GREAT things about American culture is its critique of its own excesses. Like gems hidden in plain sight, the culture brims with funny, satirical, ironic, direct and discrete artifacts that offer checks and balances to its edginess on all sides. Get too far to the right and you're a headline on the *Daily Show*; too far to the left and you're fodder for Rush Limbaugh; too narcissistic and you're dubbed another Paris Hilton; too obsessed with piety and you're lampooned for seeing saints' faces on cinnamon buns.

Among the excesses in American life is complexity. The sheer expansion of access to communication and the technology that links us is largely responsible. The amount of new information and knowledge available to us today is staggering. We have so many more options and choices than our grandparents, and the crises and threats to our security seem constantly at our door. So, wouldn't it stand to reason that the more we embrace the complex life, the better? Who'd want a simple life if you can have one that has layer upon layer of physical, social and emotional complexity? If "some" is good, isn't "more" better?

What do we see and hear from the culture, then, about life that is *not* simple; when our time is so compromised by obligations that choices evaporate; when our drive to keep up with the latest trends puts a ridiculous strain on our inability to enjoy what we have; when the tangle of debt, work and activities of daily living become so complex that we meet ourselves coming and going? And in what ways does the culture nudge us back toward a more sensible life where we live within our means, consciously choose what we want to access in the world of communications, consider the needs of others as equal to our own and value the health of the planet.

My premise is that our culture provides a living dialogue on the issue of a balanced life. Certainly, the allure of having it all, as interpreted by commercialism, is there in front of us every time we turn on the television, read print advertisements or go shopping. There are, however, subtle and overt messages inviting us to consider the simple life. William James, the father of American psychology, advanced the idea that we can't think our way into a new kind of living; rather, we must live our way into a new kind of thinking. His point is that real change isn't the result of an intellectual exercise but a holistic response to the physical, social, cognitive, emotional and spiritual experiences that move us. The barometer measuring the wisdom of change in a good direction, then, would be those indicators of health and well-being that are universally recognized: inner peace and contentment, supportive and enjoyable relationships; engagement in meaningful actions that bring about good for oneself, family, friends, communities and our global neighbors. The outcomes of living this kind of life are happiness, well-functioning families and systems that work well for citizens and the natural environment.

We are living in our generation's own unique set of crises and challenges. Economic climates and political unrest, whether local or global, generate forces that are dynamic and far reaching. They respond to the excesses of entire countries, the depletion of resources, the moral behavior of leaders and citizens and to natural phenomena. Culture, then, becomes an important compass for alerting us all to a need for adjustment or change. How so?

Culture is the "cultivation" of social life and, as such, a living, growing dynamic of interchange among expressions of human thought and behavior. The artifacts of culture are art, science and technology and legal, moral and religious systems. It is evident in rituals, customs, traditions, trends, architecture, fashion, music, literature, dance, visual art and cuisine.

Pop culture is what we call the current manifestation of this dynamic interchange of the forces of excess and complexity. *CBS Sunday Morning* ran a piece recently on the British artist Damien Hirst who has devalued his own work by producing too much of it. Galleries that sell his art have been forced to bid high for his work at auctions just to protect their investment in his name and in the pieces already in their inventory — clearly, in this case, less is more.

Additionally, the slow food movement evolved as a counterpoint to the culture of fast food, with slow food restaurants now recognizing a particular niche of customers who no longer want to eat on the run. In the arena of art, films like *The Bucket List* deal with the subject of death and trying to squeeze in all that two men hadn't taken time to do before they knew death was imminent. Music can be a particularly poignant way to critique a culture of excess. The Harry Chapin tune, "The Cat's in the Cradle," is a great example. A son laments the lack of time that his dad has to spend with him, only to have his own busyness as an adult create the same excuse for not spending time with his aging father. The sample of lyrics below brings home the point:

> A child arrived just the other day, He came to the world in the usual way. But there were planes to catch, and bills to pay. He learned to walk while I was away. And he was talking 'fore I knew it, and as he grew, He'd say, "I'm gonna be like you, dad. You know I'm gonna be like you.
>
> And the cat's in the cradle and the silver spoon, Little boy blue and the man in the moon. "When you coming home, dad?" "I don't know when, But we'll get together then. You know we'll have a good time then."
>
> I've long since retired and my son's moved away. I called him up just the other day. I said, "I'd like to see you if you don't mind." He said, "I'd love to, dad, if I could find the time. You see, my new job's a hassle, and the kid's got the flu, But it's sure nice talking to you, dad. It's been sure nice talking to you." And as I hung up the phone, it occurred to me, He'd grown up just like me. My boy was just like me.

Each generation has its own critiques etched in the art, music, poetry, novels, films, fashion, cuisine, architecture and toys of its day. Though none of these are necessary for the physical survival of individuals, I believe that they are all critical to the survival of the human soul and society as a whole. These artifacts of culture afford us an opportunity to both shape and respond to our surroundings, the ups and downs of life, and the events of history. They are the navigational system for the human family that corrects the course of human action and ultimately attempts to steer each generation successfully through its unique period of time. What can we do to foster the continued creation of culture?

In the mid-20th century, the German philosopher Josef Pieper wrote in *Leisure, the Basis of Culture* that leisure is the basis of the best that culture can produce:

> Leisure is a mental and spiritual attitude…not the result of spare time…it is an attitude of the mind, a condition of the soul…it implies an inward calm, of silence. It means not being "busy," but letting things happen. Leisure is a form of silence, of that silence which is the prerequisite of the apprehension of reality. Only the silent hear, and those who do not remain silent do not hear…. Silence here does not mean noiselessness; it means more nearly that the soul's power to answer to the reality of the world is left undisturbed. For leisure is a receptive attitude of mind, a contemplative attitude, and it is not only the occasion but also the capacity for steeping oneself in the whole of creation. Furthermore, there is a certain serenity in leisure…it is for those who are open to everything; not for those who grab and grab hold, but of those who leave the reins loose and who are free and easy themselves…. Leisure is only pos-

sible when a [person] is at one with himself... it is a [person's] happy and cheerful affirmation of his own being.

Leisure here isn't idleness; it's the freedom to become our true selves. It's a freedom that is made possible by lifestyles that afford more time for thoughtful reflection and creativity. It gives us opportunities to observe our surroundings more acutely aware of the red flags pointing to excesses of all kinds. Leisure, when valued not as a commodity but an expression of our deepest human capability, is the ultimate balancing act.

If we can live our way into a new kind of thinking, it will take more careful and intentional use of time, and a freedom with that time, that heightens our awareness of who we really are in relation to the type of person that the world tells us we are. The words of Robert Louis Stevenson echo in relevance across the century and a half since they were written. We keep our souls alive by knowing who we are in our core of being. The artifacts of leisure are there as our guideposts, balancing the messages and images of consumerism, materialism and the complex life against something more humble, simple and profound. If we can, as the ancient Buddha encouraged, find that middle way, we will be able to retain our souls. As the 18th-century Shakers sang, "'tis a gift to be simple, 'tis a gift to be free, 'tis a gift to come down where you ought to be. And when you find yourself in the place that's right, you'll be in the valley of love and delight."

"...and All the Trees of the Field Will Clap Their Hands"

by Michael Schut

MICHAEL SCHUT is Economic and Environmental Affairs Officer for The Episcopal Church; prior to that, he served at Earth Ministry for 11 years. His books include *Money and Faith: The Search for Enough; Simpler Living, Compassionate Life: A Christian Perspective;* and *Food and Faith: Justice, Joy and Daily Bread.* Michael lives in Seattle and enjoys backpacking, hiking, climbing, live music, dancing and hanging out with his nephew Carter. He has a BS in Biology and a MS in Environmental Studies.

Earth seems to be a reality that is developing with the simple aim of celebrating the joy of existence.
— THOMAS BERRY AND BRIAN SWIMME,
THE UNIVERSE STORY

IN THE PROLOGUE to *The Universe Story*, Berry and Swimme suggest that human activities in the 20th century have ended the 67-million-year venture called the Cenozoic era. Our future will be "worked out in the tensions between those committed to the Technozoic, a future of increased exploration of Earth as resource, all for the benefit of humans, and those committed to the Ecozoic, a new mode

148

of human-Earth relations, one where the well-being of the entire Earth community is the primary concern."

I want to share a story, one that for me hints at this new mode of "human-Earth relations" to which Berry refers. My hope is that, in the telling of this story, your memory and senses might recall a moment in your life when you too felt you were living closer to the Ecozoic era than the Techno-zoic, closer to health and relationship than exploitation and disconnection.

A Yosemite Sandwich

I spent the summer and early fall of 1992 leading wilderness backpacking and rock-climbing trips for Sierra Treks. After co-leading trips in the Northern Cascade's Glacier Peak Wilderness Area and Yosemite's backcountry, I had the job of supplying a group with food and gear halfway through their ten-day backpacking trip. I was to meet this Fuller Seminary student group 15 miles in on the fourth night of their trip.

I awoke early the morning of the third day of their trip, packed the faded yellow Chevy Suburban with 180 pounds of food and gear and hooked up the horse trailer. The evening before had been spent in the pasture, cornering our pack animals, Alex and Ama; I now led these long-haired, oft-stubborn llamas into the trailer's adjacent stalls. State highway gave way to backcountry gravel roads as I drove carefully to the trailhead. Unloading Alex and Ama, cinching, adjusting, tightening their packs, loading 90 pounds onto each of them and hoisting my own pack, we set off on the trail.

The mid-September day was crisp, dry and clear, comfortable for shorts and a tee-shirt. The trail took us first through a broad, mid-elevation valley grazed by a local rancher's livestock. The valley floor heaved, narrowed and steepened, and grass gave way to pine forest, white rock walls and talus slopes. Quaking golden aspen leaves held my eye and the sun's light. In late afternoon, the llamas and I descended and crossed a dry creek bed, scrambled up the opposite bank and found a spacious flat bench for the night.

I fed and tethered the llamas close by, then cooked my own gourmet pasta dinner. The day's last challenge remained: find a "bear tree" with limbs strong enough to bear (so to speak) 180 pounds of food. But, though I was not above treeline, all the trees at that elevation were simply not stout enough. I could only think of one other option: make myself into a particularly attractive bear sandwich. The seminarians were counting on me. So, I figured I could either stash the bags way outside of camp and hope they would go undisturbed...or, have them close enough to hear any midnight snacking and scare away any revelers. So I made a sandwich.

That done, I rolled out my bag and climbed in. In spite of all those food bags surrounding me, I was absolutely at peace, content, comfortably nestled between Earth, rock, tree and star. I slept well — and entertained no visitors.

An Unexpected Grace

The next morning I awoke, ate a quick breakfast, loaded Alex and Ama with those lovely intact food bags, became a beast of burden myself and continued on the trail. We passed from the Hoover Wilderness area into Yosemite's backcountry. By late afternoon, we found the group camped on an island of grass, rock and tree in the middle of Rainbow Canyon.

After spending a few days rock climbing and summiting Tower Peak with them, I donned my pack, loaded Alex and Ama, and set off for the trailhead. Again the day was bright, warm and invigorating. The air, though, snapped with cool-ness and the promise of winter.

It was toward the end of this 15-mile hike that a transfor-mative moment of intense clarity graced my life. In a way, it is so simple and perhaps so brief a moment that it is hard to describe. I was simply descending out of the high coun-try and approaching the valley below. We had just passed through a grey and white boulder-strewn talus field and then a thick willow stand. From behind, late afternoon sun rays streamed to Earth.

A large grove of young aspen trees grandly and quietly presented themselves ahead of us. Perhaps one thousand aspens were gathered there, close ranked, crowding the hard-packed trail; none of them measuring more than two to three inches in diameter, perhaps 10 to 15 feet tall. Touched by a light breeze, each leaf reflected hues of silver, of gold. As I entered that chorus of aspen tree and color, I left behind all self-consciousness, all worry, all distraction. The leaving of such cares was itself unconscious as I felt transfixed in this presence, overtaken by beauty and a sudden unveiling of the unending dance and song of creation!

I felt like royalty. It was almost as if that grove of aspens had parted, just then, allowing me to pass on the narrow trail. But there was no sense of separation, no hierarchy between me and the quaking aspen. The newness and joy, the peace and "kingliness," seemed a gift bestowed simply and directly to me from that golden grove. It seemed that their golden-leafed garments swayed silently in the breeze as their smooth, silver, slender trunks bowed in respect, recognition and celebration of relationship. I smiled on the outside and bowed on the inside, seeing more clearly than ever before their absolute beauty and rooted freedom in be-ing who they were created to be. We acknowledged each other. I felt we were dancing, laughing and celebrating.

Looking back on that hike, I wonder if for that brief moment I was given the grace to see, feel and join in creation's song of praise. Perhaps I experienced a taste of the prophet Isaiah's proclamation: "You will go out in joy and be led forth in peace; the mountains and hills will burst into song before you, and all the trees of the field will clap their hands" (Isaiah 55:12).

The experience was a moment of surprise, a moment of self-forgetfulness, placing my life and concerns in a much larger perspective. For me, to be open to such times, whether in community or solitude, whether in the city or wilderness, is to be open to awe and amazement; my response, finally, ultimately, is joy, humility and gratitude.

Earth is "a reality that is developing with the simple aim of celebrating the joy of existence," as Thomas Berry suggested. This experience with the aspens is one of my more poignant moments of participation in that celebration. My mind frequently travels back to that hike and the moments of timeless grace: grace because I did not seek out such an experience; it was all a gift, timeless as only self-forgetfulness and intense relationship can be.

[Note: This essay originally appeared in Earth Ministry's *Earth Letter*, May 1996.]

Decluttering

by Sarah Susanka

An acclaimed architect, SARAH SUSANKA is the best-selling author of eight books, including *The Not So Big House* and *The Not So Big Life*. In her *Not So Big House* series of books, Sarah has helped readers understand that the sense of "home" they're seeking has almost nothing to do with quantity and everything to do with quality. She points out that we feel "at home" in our *houses* when the place where we live reflects who we are in our personal, inner world. In *The Not So Big Life*, she uses this same set of notions to explain that we can feel "at home" in our *lives* only when the way we live reflects the truth of who we are in our hearts.

IT'S BEEN A LITTLE over a month since I wrote a blog entry — a month in which I have been attempting to "vacate" after an intense three months of book promotion. It was an enlightening time, spurred on by a call from a reporter from the *Wall Street Journal*, June Fletcher, who told me she was contributing to an article about what a number of well-known individuals planned to do with their summers, and then whether or not they followed through. She wanted to include me amongst her list of celebrities, and so she asked me, "What are you planning to do? Do you have a task in mind that you want to accomplish, and if so why this one?"

I knew the answer as soon as she asked. Each time I was interviewed by phone about *The Not So Big Life* and the parallels between how we inhabit our houses and our lives, I had been painfully aware that my inner office — the place in which I write, meditate and talk to reporters — was filled (discreetly, of course) with boxes that I had brought from my previous house in St. Paul, but had not yet unpacked. That was four years ago! It was time for some decluttering, time to go through the boxes and find out what needed to be tossed and what was worth keeping.

When I sold my St. Paul house, I was already living in Raleigh, NC, and was busy with my writing career. So busy in fact that I didn't have time to go to St. Paul and sort through everything myself. Instead I had a good friend, who had been house-sitting for me for three years, oversee the process of packing and transporting all my St. Paul possessions — no small undertaking, I might add. They had arrived in the middle of my writing my fourth book, *Home by Design*, and so rather than unpacking right then, I figured I'd wait for a month or two, until I had time.

Well, you guessed it, that time never seemed to arrive. There was always another project requiring my attention, and the unpacking process, which I knew would likely take a week or two, was way down the list of priorities. June Fletcher's simple query provided the impetus I needed to make a dedicated effort to undertake the long-delayed unpacking.

I spent a couple of hours a day for most of my month off, and still there's more to be done, but the part of the task that most effects my everyday life, the removal of all those descreetly concealed cardboard boxes, has been accomplished. There's a lot more space underneath the countertops that flank my inner office now, more breathing space and a lot less clutter. But there's something else as well — a revelation that came about only as a result of all that unpacking. And I now see that this was the real point of the exercise — the meaningful benefit.

What fascinated me was that my lifelong delight in writing has provided a sort of lens through which to see how interests have grown and developed over the years. Amongst all the unnecessary junk and clutter were some true treasures — written in journals, on legal pads, and in three-ring binders that extend back to when I first moved to this country in 1971 at 14. I had not realized before how many of the things I write about today were interests even in my teens and early twenties. I wrote about the strange absence of community that I experienced when we first moved to a suburb of Los Angeles. And I wondered, in the script of an English schoolgirl, why people built houses where so many of the rooms were, as far as I could tell, never used. I pondered the possibility of a different way of designing and of living — one more focused on quality than quantity.

I no longer remember writing these things, and I haven't looked at them since I wrote them, over 30 years ago now, but there's a clear flavor to all of them that is very recognizably the same voice that is writing through my fingertips today. I suppose this shouldn't be so surprising, but I'd had the impression that, with all the intervening years, I'd learned something, grown wiser perhaps. These early writings would suggest not. They seem to indicate that what I say today was already latent and observable in the conjectures of my teenage self.

If we all had this potential to look back through our lives and see what we were thinking back then, I have a feeling we'd all be able to see similar themes running, like veins of some precious mineral. It's a pretty amazing discovery — slightly deflating on the one hand as I saw how little I had changed, but simultaneously thrilling as I recognized the characteristics of the flavor of expression that runs through everything I've touched for the past three or four decades.

This insight was topped off by a phone conversation I had with my high-school English teacher whom I mention in the book. "So, you've finally written the book you were planning when you were in my sophomore English class," he declared. "I have?" I responded. He told me that even at 14 I was talking about writing a book describing a different and more conscious way of living, in which everything that happens is seen as a part of one's education as a student of life. I nearly fell off my chair. I have no recollection of this, but it supports the thesis that we hold within us from the beginning, the seeds of everything that plays out in our adult lives.

I see now that the real lesson of my decluttering task was not that I needed to throw everything out, but that, through the process of sorting, reviewing and culling, I was able to render down the important ingredients of my life into its particular and unique flavor, just as one would do in the kitchen with a fine sauce. It's all there already. We just have to take the time to let it simmer, and then after decades have past, to taste the results. I highly recommend it. I've learned a lot.

And finally, a question for you to ponder — If you were able to look back through your life and see your past thoughts, interests and passions, what do you think you would discover about yourself? What's the flavor of expression running through you? Is there some physical, mental or emotional decluttering that you could do that would help you to discover this flavor? Write and let me know what you discover.

Wabi-Sabi Time

by Robyn Griggs Lawrence

ROBYN GRIGGS LAWRENCE is the editor-in-chief of *Natural Home* (naturalhomemagazine.com), a bimonthly magazine that helps readers craft healthy, serene homes and lifestyles. Robyn has written and spoken nationally on topics ranging from eco-building to spiritual design. She lives in Boulder, Colorado, with her two children, Stacey, 14, and Cree, 10.

Robyn grew up in Iowa, where she fell in love with the old, weathered barns that dot the grasslands. Her father, a woodworker, instilled in her a love of fine, simple craftsmanship and design integrity. She combined this background with a penchant for Japanese aesthetics and culture in her book, *The Wabi-Sabi House*, which introduces readers to the ancient Japanese art of finding beauty in things that are imperfect, impermanent, rustic and primitive. Lawrence discovered wabi-sabi nearly a decade ago, while visiting a rustic stone house in rural Maine on assignment for *Natural Home*. As soon as the homeowner introduced her to the concept, she had an "aha" moment — this is how she's decorated and lived all her life. She believes wabi-sabi is an important means of helping people accept and embrace their homes as sacred, nurturing spaces — just the way they are.

Enduring poverty in life
I prepare fire on the hearth
and enjoy the profound touch of Tea.

— MATUO BASHO

M Y FIRST ARTICLES on wabi-sabi were published right around 9/11. At that time, the Japanese philosophy of finding beauty in the imperfect had a serious underground following, but the concept was new to most. I'd recently discovered wabi-sabi, which to me seemed a great umbrella for a lot of the conversations getting under way at that time: Simplicity, slow food, recycling and reuse. In the first where-do-we-go-now months after the planes hit the towers, I thought Americans might go the wabi way, toward Victory Gardens and plainer living. Instead, we went for easy credit and patriotic shopping; wabi-sabi had to wait.

Hard knocks change a nation. Wealth ebbs and flows, thrift and greed take turns in our cycling consciousness. After 9/11, we shopped. Seven years later, we stopped. "It's the end of the era of conspicuous displays of wealth," historian Steve Fraser told the *New York Times* in October 2008. "We are entering a new chapter in our history."

Wabi-sabi time.

Wabi-sabi is an ancient Japanese philosophy with roots in Zen, revering austerity, nature and the everyday. It stems more directly from the Japanese tea ceremony, a simple Zen ritual for making and sharing a cup of tea — an approach that warlords in 15th-century Japan turned into a means of showing off their immense wealth through gaudy tea houses and imported goods. The wabi way of tea (*wabichado*) grew out of a backlash to that, championed by a master so powerful that his style is practiced to this day. Sen no Rikyu's quiet, simple tea ceremony, with tea served in locally fired bowls and flowers in fishermen's baskets, quickly became the most sought-after way to have tea. Wood and bamboo replaced porcelain, and lacquer and hospitality trumped pretension as the height of taste.

The name for Rikyu's style of tea, wabi, is a poet's word. It's a little bit melancholy; one of my favorite descriptions is "the feeling you have when you're waiting for your lover." It describes a little monk in his torn robe, enjoying a night by the fire — content in poverty. The status of these monks rose alongside wabi in 15th-century Japan, as people grew war-weary, and the upper classes grew tired of conspicuous consumption. Simplicity — the aesthetic of the everyday samurai — took on a new nobility. And no matter how much wealth they had, everyone in Japan could make and share a cup of tea.

No one's quite sure how the word "sabi" got hooked up with "wabi," (or even when that happened), but the two conjoined took wabi a step further. "Sabi" means "the bloom of time," connoting tarnish and rust, the enchantment of old things. It brings appreciation for dignified, graceful aging: worn cobblestones, weathered wood, oxidized silver. Paired with "wabi," it became a moniker for a philosophy that reveres age, imperfection and natural order.

But we don't practice tea in modern America; we drink coffee. So how does this translate? Like all good philosophies, it gives us a launching point toward thinking about what matters. Wabi-sabi says we can take pleasure in ending the spending spree and feel good about frugality. It lets us celebrate the beauty in just getting by — something a lot of us crave right now.

In his sacred tea text, *Nanporoku*, Sen no Rikyu wrote: "A luxurious house and the taste of delicacies are only pleasures of the mundane world. It is enough if the house does not leak and the food keeps hunger away." Sage advice that stands the test of time. We can start developing our own *wabigokoro*, or wabi mind and heart, in our homes.

Wabibitos live modestly, satisfied with things as they are. They own only what's necessary for its utility or beauty (ideally, both). They revere humans over machines, surrounding themselves with things that resonate with the spirit of their makers. Wabi-sabi is imperfect: a beloved chipped vase or a scarred wooden table.

This getting-away-from-perfect is one of wabi-sabi's most appealing facets. It means you can keep the tablecloth even though it's fraying on the edges and admire the rug as it fades from brilliant red to pale rose. You can let things be. It's like going to Grandma's house.

Our Depression-era grandmothers knew wabi-sabi. And their houses were so comfortable because they understood, inherently, the difference between wabi and slobby. Their tablecloths and linens were faded, but they never had rips or tears. Their furnishings had a settled-in quality, but they weren't dilapidated. Their floors showed wear, but they were always swept, with rag rugs that wove together memories in their use of old garments.

We can't order that warmth and comfort through a catalog or online — regardless of our household budget. Like all good things, wabi-sabi is more about time than money. It's about taking the time and having the perspective to find beauty in things as they are. One of my personal heroes, Elizabeth Gordon — who was at the helm of *House Beautiful* throughout the mid-20th century — once wrote, "If you can't find beauty — for free — when you are poor, you won't be likely to have it when you are rich…even though you may have bought and paid for it."

Gordon often railed against conspicuous beauty, which was rife in the prosperous '50s. "When a thing is self-consciously made to be beautiful (as though beauty was the total aim) it never seems to work, and it becomes futile and knick-knacky," she wrote. "There has to be some purpose and usefulness about the creating." A Japanophile, she was translating for Americans the principle of *yo-no-bi*, defining beauty by its utility. The Japanese call this hidden beauty a thing's "ah-ness."

One of the first lessons of the wabi tea ceremony is to find and admire the beauty in every utensil, from the bamboo water scoop to the tea bowl. Several tea masters I've met have suggested bringing this reverence to items you use every day — maybe your coffee mug. Christy Bartlett, a San Francisco-based tea master who represents the family of Rikyu's descendants, does this with a tea bowl she's had for 22 years. "Every time I look at it, I still see something new," she said. But to do this, she warned, "You can't be lazy. It's up to you to see and see something new, to sustain your interest in the world around you. It's not up to the world to entertain you. It requires effort to be interested."

That probably means turning off the TV — maybe the hardest first step toward a wabi-sabi lifestyle.

Wabi-sabi has made inroads in Western culture time and again; strains of it can be seen in the lifestyles of the Puritans, the Shakers and the Transcendentalists. It showed up in Arts and Crafts furnishings (a reaction to the overwrought Victorian era) and even in Eames chairs (simple, functional design for the masses).

Wabi-sabi is a logical reaction to a society disgusted with its own excess. (William Morris, father of the Arts and Crafts movement, often railed against the "swinish luxury of the rich," and many of his lectures could be used on the campaign trail today.) But the beauty in it is that it's not a bitter condemnation — it's a change in perspective. Instead of buying, we could make things. We could grow our own. We could put away the credit cards.

We could start by taking on the most important tenet of the tea: *ichigo, ichie*, or "once in a lifetime." This reminds us that every meeting is a once-in-a-lifetime occasion to enjoy good company, beautiful art and a cup of tea. We never know what might happen tomorrow, or even later today. But in the moment, we could stop to share conversation and a cup of tea. And that sure beats the bad news on TV.

Changing the World
One Block at a Time

by Jay Walljasper

JAY WALLJASPER, author of *The Great Neighborhood Book*, writes and speaks widely about community revitalization, travel and contemporary issues. The editor of *Utne Reader* magazine for 15 years, he is now editor of OnTheCommons.org, a senior fellow at Project for Public Spaces and editor-at-large of *Ode* magazine. From an early age, simply living struck Jay as being more fun. His website is JayWalljasper.com.

T HE NEIGHBORHOOD is the basic building block of human society, and practical efforts to save the planet start right there. Whether a rural village in India, a suburban subdivision in California or a bohemian quarter in Berlin, neighborhoods shape people's lives in powerful and surprising ways.

Like a lot of journalists, I was slow in recognizing these facts. I spent so much time looking into promising events everywhere else in the world, from Eastern Europe to Silicon Valley, that I overlooked positive possibilities of my own backyard in Minneapolis.

I finally realized what I was missing, ironically, a long way from my home. My wife Julie and I spent a week in

Paris on our honeymoon, arriving with big plans to cover every inch of the city from the modern towers of La Defense to the Arab district around Rue du Faubourg du Temple. Yet we found ourselves passing entire days within just a few blocks of our hotel in the Latin Quarter. We'd stroll the boulevards, buy lunch in a street market, wander through the Luxembourg Gardens and while away the evenings in sidewalk cafés. We agreed the Pompidou Centre and Versailles could wait for another trip. We were immersed in the life of our "urban village."

Even the greatest and most cosmopolitan cities are simply patchworks of lively and distinct neighborhoods. Each arrondissement of Paris has its own town hall, usually with a nearby plaza or café where Parisians gather to hear local gossip and bump into their neighbors — not so different from the square of a small town.

As humans, we possess an innate drive to seek out familiar faces and to belong somewhere, which can be traced back to our evolutionary origins in tribal communities. But that doesn't stop us from reaching out to the wider world, an equally strong natural urge. You can see these two primal human needs peacefully coexisting whenever you enter a coffee shop. You always find people tapping at their laptops, but also striking up conversations with someone at the next table. Even the most enthusiastic planetary networkers, people who pass their days swapping information with colleagues in Hong Kong and text messaging new MySpace friends in New Zealand, crave face-to-face contact with fellow local denizens.

The mark of the 21st-century person is to have one foot in the world and one foot squarely planted in their community. Even as our intellectual and economic horizons expand, the local community is still where we lead our lives, where our toes touch the ground, where everybody knows our name. Experience has taught me that being rooted in the neighborhood of your choice (which may be many times zones from the neighborhood where you grew up) offers not just comfort and pleasure, but a prime opportunity to make a difference in your community — and the world.

Like most newlyweds, Julie and I came home from our honeymoon with thoughts of buying a house. And, of course, we sought a place that had the feel of Paris, even if it was a Midwestern tavern on the corner instead of a sidewalk café. The problem was that many other folks around town had the same idea, and all the neighborhoods that attracted us were out of our price range. So we stayed put for more than four years in a one-bedroom apartment in Minneapolis's lively Uptown district, which did feel like an urban village to us.

Finally we fell in love with an old house, brimming with natural woodwork and turn-of-the-20th-century charm, and took the plunge. Our new neighborhood, Kingfield, was pleasant, with tree-lined streets and well-built homes, but the noticeable lack of street life made moving there feel a bit like exile. When a burglar broke into our house in broad daylight just a few months later, brazenly eating a bowl of cereal at the kitchen table before leaving with our valuables, we wondered if we'd made a terrible mistake.

Luckily, we fell in with a group of neighbors, mostly newcomers like us, who got together on Friday nights for potluck suppers. We would trade stories about remodeling projects and backyard gardens as well as our desire for more places to go and things to do in Kingfield. We also compared notes on the nagging crime problem. These discussions eventually led us to get involved with local issues — especially after the city unveiled plans to widen an already busy street in the neighborhood, which would mean faster, more dangerous traffic and declining property values. Julie soon became the president of the neighborhood board, and we regularly joined our friends at public meetings to voice our visions for the future Kingfield.

Gradually we watched Kingfield change, bearing a closer resemblance to the urban village where we dreamed of living. The proposal to widen the avenue was defeated, thanks to the efforts of people from many neighborhoods, and our success became an inspiration to other people around town opposing wrongheaded road projects. New businesses, including a number of cafés, opened. Citizen safety initiatives along with increasing street life helped reduce the crime rate. Today, Kingfield sports a farmers' market, reinvigorated business districts, local arts shows, housing improvements in its low-income blocks and new community anchors for the growing Latino population.

Julie and I, and our son Soren, can now stroll around to corner to the sidewalk tables at Caffe Tempo for a croissant or ice cream cone — something that's possible only because we and dozens of neighbors turned out for a public meeting where we demanded that zoning rules be amended so the café could open. I now proudly tell people I live in Kingfield, rather than "someplace south of Uptown," and many of them nod approvingly.

Ever since my teens, I have been involved in a number of environmental causes, ranging from national political campaigns to international green initiatives. Out of these efforts — some successful and most of them at least inspiring — nothing has yielded the lasting results and been more fun than what's happened in my neighborhood. Issues that seem overwhelming at the national or even municipal level — such as climate change or sprawl — can be effectively tackled close to home. That's because the people who live in a particular locale are the experts on that place, with the wisdom and commitment to get things done.

Neighborhood activism is sometimes cast as a narrow, even selfish pursuit. There's a hole in the ozone layer, and people are starving in Africa, and you're obsessed with starting a farmer's market! But that ignores one of the key assets of 21st-century life. Thanks to our amazing global communications networks, no good idea stays local for long. The success of that farmer's market and the growers who sell meat and vegetables there, for instance, might someday offer practical information for nutrition projects in the developing world. (Incidentally, most people I've met who are involved in neighborhood issues are also active in broader social causes, with the local work inspiring their global perspective, and vice versa.)

It's now easier than ever to "Think globally," as the old saying goes, and "Act locally." Here are some examples of neighborhood success stories, which could be applied in many places around the planet:

- Grandmothers at the Yesler Terrace public housing project in Seattle drove drug dealers from their community by camping out in lawn chairs at street corners notorious for crack traffic. They simply sat there knitting, and the dealers soon cleared out, proving that frail old grannies willing to speak up for their neighborhood can sometimes accomplish more than dozens of cops in squad cars. This idea that ordinary people prevent crime by taking back the streets has been successfully tried in many other communities.

- A group of frustrated neighbors in Delft, Netherlands, finally took action about autos speeding down their street. They dragged old couches and tables into the middle of the road, strategically arranging them so that motorists could still pass — but only if they drove slowly. The police eventually arrived and had to admit that this scheme, although clearly illegal, was a good idea. Soon the city was installing its own devices to slow traffic, and the idea of traffic calming was born — an innovative solution that is used across the globe to make streets safer.

- In Porto Alegre, Brazil, (population 1.3 million) local officials enlist the wisdom of neighborhood residents in figuring out how to best apportion their tax money. Citizens gather in neighborhood assemblies to decide what's needed in their part of town, and then elect representatives to advise the city council on budget priorities. This "participatory budget" has been credited with lowering unemployment, improving sanitary conditions and revitalizing Porto Alegre's poor neighborhoods. More than 1,200 cities across the world have now adopted the idea.

- In the Harmony Village community of Golden, Colorado — a fast-growing suburb west of Denver — neighbors meet for breakfast once a month to trade ideas and share resources for fighting global warming and other environmental threats. Dan Chiras, who welcomes everyone into his kitchen for coffee and conversation, outlined what they've been able to accomplish in his book *Superbia*:

  > [The group] proposed Harmony Village residents install solar panels on the roofs of their homes, and that the village use energy efficient compact fluourescent bulbs in outdoor fixtures. They routinely write letters to politicians and recently saved a nearby piece of land that was slated for development.

- In Portland, Oregon, more than 100 residents of the Boundary Street Neighborhood have worked together to restore native plants along the banks of their local creek. "We've tapped into neighborhood expertise — one guy has a PhD in biology," notes Dick Roy, one of the organizers. "We've taken advantage of all the good energy to make our neighborhood more environmentally stable."

- In the Toronto suburb of Mississauga, Dave Marcucci built a bench in his frontyard as a way of bringing people together. This raised eyebrows up and down the block. "Why aren't you putting the bench in the backyard where you can enjoy it?" neighbors asked. "This bench is for you," he replied. When the bench was ready, Marcucci threw a party, inviting everyone to come sit on it. From that point on, his neighborhood was never the same. Older people took to walking around the block again, because they had a place to stop and rest. Kids sat on it waiting for the school bus. Even his skeptical neighbors have been won over. A family around the corner has installed a bench in their own front yard as a spot for people to gather.

The Real Wealth
of Neighborhoods

by Dave Wann

DAVID WANN is an author, filmmaker and speaker about sustainable design and sustainable lifestyles. His most recent book, *Simple Prosperity: Finding Real Wealth in a Sustainable Lifestyle*, is a sequel to the best-selling book he co-authored, *Affluenza: The All-Consuming Epidemic*, which is now in nine languages. He's at work on a book tentatively titled *Beyond Simple Choices: 100 Value-driven Decisions for a Sustainable World*.

David is the father of two children, president of the Sustainable Futures Society and a fellow of the national Simplicity Forum. He helped design the co-housing neighborhood where he's lived for 12 years, has taught at the college level and worked more than a decade for the US Environmental Protection Agency.

WE USE THE question, "Where do you live?" automatically, without really thinking about it. Sometimes the question just means, How far do I have to drive to get there, and how long will it take? Too often "where you live" means where you park your car, consume energy, watch three or four hours of TV a day, generate four pounds of trash and argue with your spouse. Hopefully, in *your* case, it means something far more magnificent: where you have your best relationships, and your most creative ideas. Where you feel the most content and energized. Where you *come to life*.

Ideally, where you live is about a *place* and not just a house. A place where neighbors know and value you enough to be there for you if you need help, and where you can meet the universal human need to offer your own support and caring. A great place to walk, because a thriving pedestrian population results in healthy neighbors, cleaner air, human-scaled architecture and lower crime. A great neighborhood creates less stress and offers more social capital and trust than a typical neighborhood, and it creates less stress on the environment by using less land, water, energy and fewer materials. While the general assumption is that a house in the upscale part of town would always be preferable, it may not necessarily have the most value overall. To afford that mini-mansion you may be stretching your paycheck tighter than the rubber band on a toy airplane, spending many hours vacuuming unused rooms and climbing ladders to squeegee endless, impossible-to-reach windows.

If we think about what we need to be happy, great neighborhoods can provide many of those needs directly. We need a sense of belonging and participation, a sense of security and safety; we need healthy food, connection with the no-worries feelings that nature bestows and activities that we enjoy, to name just a few. Think of the places you've lived, and how they met or failed to meet needs like these.

I've been pretty lucky in the neighborhood department; I've spent at least half my years in places that really supported my growth. One of them was Larchmont, a small suburb of New York City with great connections. It's connected to the ocean, by passenger rail to the City and all the culture that goes with it and to a rich heritage that's reflected in its sturdy, sometimes opulent homes. It's linked with the

Boston Post Road, developed in the 1670s from an old Algonquin Indian trail that King Charles II made America's first official mail route. President Washington traveled this road through New England on his 1789 inaugural tour.

To live in Larchmont is to be into sailing, fishing or at least swimming. Chances are that the household includes commuters to jobs in the City that are stimulating — often linked with company headquarters, entertainment or the financial sector. And then there's upstate, a huge universe of forests, farms and delightful small towns that don't seem to notice that New York City's on the same planet.

I went back to Larchmont a few years ago, after 35 years away, observing again how great communities meet needs. I parked at my old house and spent a few hours walking through the old neighborhoods — even sneaking across the corner of a backyard the way I used to on my way to elementary school. I was a time traveler, on a spring day somewhere in my past. The dogwoods were in full bloom, and the houses still echoed with the voices of my friends. Munching a classic hot dog from the same stand I went to as a kid, I analyzed this place through the eyes of a filmmaker. (I'd recently produced several programs on sustainable communities.) My old hometown had great bones: well-designed pockets of public space in each neighborhood, a great school and big old hardwood trees that forested the whole village. In fact, I recognized a few familiar cracks in the heaving sidewalk in front of my old house, created years ago by wandering oak tree roots, and the same steel steps and stone walls were still securely in place at my elementary school (a kid-turned-grownup would notice).

I tested a standard indicator of a great community, walking from my old house to the business center in a little more than five minutes, which makes it quite possible to pick up a quart of milk without burning a quart of gas, and say hello to neighbors along the way. A similar indicator still seemed viable in Larchmont — an eight-year-old girl could safely walk to the park or the public library. This indicator presupposes a library worth walking to, sidewalks to walk on and neighborhoods safeguarded by the active presence of the neighbors themselves. I was tempted to try developer Andres Duany's blindfold test, in which you assume that slow-moving cars will stop if you cross a commercial street with a blindfold on. But my faith in modern-day Larchmont didn't extend *quite* that far.

I observed with older eyes that the town offered a place for people, not just cars. I observed great parks, great attention to lush landscaping, increasing ethnic diversity and the classic, fully functional railroad, still running right on schedule. To my delight, I re-experienced a town worth living in (if you could afford it), a town whose residents cared about its continuance. And I realized that community greatness is *built* on caring, good design, citizen participation and a strong vision of what a community can be. From these desirable qualities flow a strong fiscal base and a satisfied population. Yet many of America's 70,000 or more communities don't reach these goals, partly because the "factory" that builds and maintains communities (zoning regulations, building industry, government incentives, certain patterns of thinking) is out of step with what people need.

Since *Ozzie and Harriet* and *Father Knows Best* days, America's demographics and values have changed significantly, yet we are still building neighborhoods and homes that assume upwardly mobile families live there with jobs in the city and plenty of time to take care of the lawn. In fact, fewer than half of America's suburban homes (where more than half of Americans now live) are occupied by traditional mom-and-pop families; more than a quarter of our houses are occupied by single people. In *The City: A Global*

History, author Joel Kotkin points out, "Roughly three out of five jobs in American metropolitan areas are now located in the suburbs, and more than twice as many Americans commute from suburb to suburb than from suburb to city." The ethnic mix of the suburbs has changed, too, enriching the culture and diversity of its neighborhoods. For example, a majority of Asian-Americans, 50 percent of Hispanics and 40 percent of African-Americans now live in the suburbs.

Because it was assumed that Americans would always love our cars and never need to take account of how much we were consuming, builders accommodated a doubling of the US population (between 1950 and 2005) with a drive-in design strategy. The idea of community was rarely part of the equation, and streets were laid out with little thought of human needs like socializing, solar exposure and exercise. Locating the new subdivisions on cheap farmland resulted in several dysfunctions at the same time: it not only paved and smothered the region's best agricultural land but also put miles of resource-intensive travel between our houses and jobs, stores and friends

Now, we're faced with an ironic but pressing question: how do we strategically rebuild some of what we've just built to make it work better? In addition, how do we (quickly) refine the focus and priorities of new construction in the near future, because much will remain in place for hundreds of years? All new construction needs to be resource efficient, because the days of unlimited fuels, raw materials and land are over. And it needs to enrich life rather than degrade it, to be less about buying life and more about experiencing it. The cultural components of American expansion have provided various ways to escape. The TV, automobile and the suburb (country life without the mud) taught us we could always choose to be somewhere else. Consequently, we undervalue and underutilize where we already are.

Now that the brightness of the American Dream is flickering, making neighborhoods and villages livable and sustainable again should be a top priority. As we reshape *existing* components of suburbia, for example, we need to determine the best location for village centers, as well as who will fund their creation. Small businesses that convert existing houses and lots into stores is one source. Tax dollars invested in public infrastructure like community centers is another, and new alliances with utility companies may be a third. To avoid the high costs of adding power plants and water treatment plants, the utilities may fund capacity (including purchase and demolition of certain existing buildings) at the neighborhood scale. New low-impact ways of generating electricity, such as large fuel cells (with pure hydrogen as a fuel source) would work well at the neighborhood scale. Such mini-power plants could supply electricity, pure water and heat to networks of houses, generating neither pollution nor noise. This technology is still very expensive, but its value may be much larger than its cost.

Instead of spending half a trillion dollars (EPA estimate) to repair and replace sewage infrastructure in upcoming years, wastewater utilities might begin to look closely at neighborhood-scaled "living machines" that mimic the way nature purifies sewage. Snails, fish, cattails and other natural species live in tanks inside of greenhouses; the wastewater flows through them at a controlled speed. Because these systems perform as well or better than resource-intensive conventional treatment plants, some state environmental departments, such as in Indiana, have certified their use. I toured a living machine in Indiana, where wastes from about 80 employees at the PAWS office (headquarters of cartoonist Jim Davis' Garfield empire) are efficiently treated. Since decomposition is quick and natural, the facility smells as earthy and sweet as its final stage — a crop of marketable roses.

Conceivably, a neighborhood's homeowners association could become a for-profit business, leasing/owning and operating small businesses and mini-facilities that make their neighborhoods far more sustainable. As Michael Schuman suggests in the book *Going Local*, community-owned enterprises are not only possible (the Green Bay Packers is one), but seemingly inevitable. Why not invest directly in our communities? Another force to be reckoned with is the confederation of Homeowners Associations; 57 million Americans are now "citizens" of a quarter of a million private jurisdictions. What an opportunity to promote sustainability! Instead of just decreeing and enforcing what neighbors must not do (such as have sculptures on their front lawn or put up basketball hoops), imagine neighborhood associations that begin to encourage resource efficiency and the creation of neighborhood culture!

One very interesting example is the Norwood-Quince neighborhood in Boulder, Colorado, where neighbors are determined to make the car an alternative form of transportation. Resident Graham Hill is leading the charge. Expert in out-of-car experiences from electric-assisted bikes to Segway scooters, Hill and his neighbors have taken one step after another — often literally — to make their neighborhood people-friendly. Out of their 210 households, for instance, 130 have Eco-passes for the well-managed bus system. The City provides discounts for neighborhoods that participate cooperatively.

The neighbors also have excellent pedestrian access to a shopping area, open space in a nearby park, several bike-pedestrian walkways and even a solar-lit walkway paid for by a neighborhood mini-grant from the City. "We observed that many neighbors weren't walking to the Boulder Market at night because the street was too dark and seemed unsafe," explains Hill. "So we applied for a grant to install solar-powered lights with battery storage. Now foot traffic can be seen — and can see — even at night."

Forty people in the neighborhood are members in a car-share club — essentially car rental by the hour — and more than 50 have become members in an electric bike-share operation; the electric bikes are powered by solar cells incorporated into a bike shed.

The neighbors are now looking into creating better access by linking several existing pathways with easements through the edges of several private yards. To dramatize the efficiencies of muscle power versus fossil fuel power, Hill and his colleagues staged a race between the Mayor, who rode a bicycle, and the County Commissioner, who drove a hybrid car. After each ran several compulsory errands, the bike-riding mayor won.

What Makes a Neighborhood Great

Cultural Assets

Great neighborhoods have active residents, newsletters and e-mail listservs for sharing tools, tickets, civic information and good-hearted jokes. They have discussion groups, community projects like park cleanup or creek restoration, potluck dinners, volleyball games and skiing parties. (The neighbors of Elgin, Illinois, have a four-foot-tall, wooden Blue Tulip that makes monthly rounds from one yard to another. When the Tulip appears on your front lawn, it's your turn to host a Friday night neighborhood party.)

Skill sharing, tool sharing, mentoring of the young by the elderly, job referrals, daycare, dog care, neighborhood rosters with telephone numbers and e-mails; bulletin boards — these kinds of activities and tools encourage the creation of "neighbornets." (In Seattle, famous for its distinctive neighborhoods, Phinney EcoVillage — an existing neighborhood — has a Home

Alone group, a natural health group, a peace group and other networks. It has recently begun taking pledges from neighbors to fight global warming by driving less, not using dryers, using compact fluorescent bulbs, etc.)

Free entertainment, like twilight conversations in the park, wine tasting parties in someone's backyard or spontaneous, no-pressure bike rides to a landmark in the town (like an overlook, favorite bar or ice cream parlor).

Sharing of life's ups and downs. (If I let you vent your frustrations as we each get home from work, I know I have a listener when *I* need to vent. If you show me your family album, I'll show you mine.)

Neighbors who live in their house for years, creating neighborhood history and neighborhood stewards. (Studies show that hometowns are the most popular places to retire, despite all the literature about "where to retire." Of the 35 million people 65 and older who lived in the US between 1995 and 2000, only 22 percent left their homes and neighborhoods.)

Physical Assets

Community gardens on vacant lots, utility rights-of-way and land donated/lent for tax write-offs. Also, the trading of garden produce and recipes from private gardens and kitchens; and neighborhood contracts with local growers (community-supported agriculture). Information about local growers can be found at nal.usda.gov/afsic/csa.

Transportation by proximity: location, location, location and planning, planning, planning. Great neighborhoods need stores, parks, pathways, bike trails and access to public transit. (Some banks offer lower interest rates and down payments — often called location-efficient mortgages and green mortgages — to homebuyers.)

Slow, safe streets. Working with city governments, many neighborhoods have requested and received traffic circles, narrower streets, etc. Studies have shown that the speed and volume of traffic often determine the number of friends and acquaintances neighbors have, with fast, high-volume streets reducing that number by a factor of ten. In about 20 states, Safe Routes to School has won public funding to improve and safeguard sidewalks, crosswalks and bike paths that link children and their families to schools.

A gathering place in the neighborhood: a community center or possibly an HOA-owned, formerly private residence with meeting, dining, office and guest-room space. Or at least a familiar space at a library, school or church near the neighborhood.

The Speed Trap

by Jay Walljasper

JAY WALLJASPER, author of *The Great Neighborhood Book*, writes and speaks widely about community revitalization, travel and contemporary issues. The editor of *Utne Reader* magazine for 15 years, he is now editor of OnTheCommons.org, a senior fellow at Project for Public Spaces and editor-at-large of *Ode* magazine. From an early age, simply living struck Jay as being more fun. His website is JayWalljasper.com

THE ALARM RINGS and you hop out of bed. Another day is off and running. A quick shower. Wake the kids and rush them through breakfast so they won't miss the bus. Down a cup of coffee. Shovel a bowl of cornflakes. Hurry out to the car, not forgetting a swift kiss on your partner's cheek. Hightail it to the freeway, making a mental note to grab some takeout Thai on the way home. (The kids' soccer practice starts at 6:15 sharp.) Weave back and forth looking for the fastest lane while the radio deejay barks out the minutes — 8:33, 8:41, quarter to. Reaching work, you sprint into the building and leap up the stairs three at a time, arriving at your desk with seconds to spare. You take a couple of deep breaths, then remember that the project you didn't finish last night must be faxed to New York by 10:00. Meanwhile, you've got five voice-mail messages and seven more on e-mail, two of them marked urgent.

More and more it feels like our lives have turned into a grueling race toward a finish line we never reach. No matter how fast we go, no matter how many comforts we forgo in order to quicken our pace, there never seems to be enough time.

It wasn't supposed to turn out this way. As a kid in the 1960s, I remember hearing that one of the biggest challenges of the future would be what to do with all our time. Amazing inventions were going to free up great stretches of our days for what really matters: friends, family, fun. But just the opposite has happened. We've witnessed a proliferation of dazzling time-saving innovations — jet travel, personal computers, Fed Ex, cellphones, microwaves, drive-through restaurants, home shopping networks, the World Wide Web — yet the pace of life has been cranked to a level that would have been unimaginable three decades ago.

Curiously, there has been scant public discussion about this dramatic speed-up of society. People may complain about how busy they are, how overloaded modern life has become, but speed is still viewed as generally positive — something that will help us all enrich our lives. Journalists, business leaders, politicians and professors feed our imaginations with visions of the new world of instantaneous communications and high-speed travel. Even many activists who are skeptical of the wonders of modern progress, the folks who patiently remind us that small is beautiful and less is more, look on speed as an undeniable asset in achieving a better society. Four-hundred-mile-an-hour trains, they assure us, will curtail pollution, and modem links across the planet will promote human rights.

Revving up the speed, in fact, is often heralded as the answer to problems caused by our overly busy lives. Swamped by the accelerating pace of work? Get a computer that's faster. Feel like your life is spinning out of control? Increase your efficiency by learning to read and write faster. No time to enjoy life? Purchase any number of products advertised on television that promise to help you make meals faster, exercise faster and finish all your time-consuming errands faster.

Yet it seems that the faster we go, the farther we fall behind. Not only in the literal sense of not getting done what we set out to do, but at a deeper level too. I feel this keenly in my own life. Like many Americans, I've always moved at a fast clip. I can't stand small talk, waiting in line or slow numbers on the dance floor. It has always seemed obvious to me that the faster I move, the more things I can do and the more fun and meaning my life will have. But it has gotten to the point where my days, crammed with all sorts of activities, feel like an Olympic endurance event: the everyday-athon. As I race through meals, work, family time, social encounters and the physical landscape on my way to my next appointment, I'm beginning to wonder what I've been missing, what pleasures I've been in too much of a hurry to appreciate or even notice.

I hear an invisible stopwatch ticking even when I'm supposed to be having fun. A few weeks ago, I promised myself a visit to a favorite used-book store that I hadn't stopped in for a while. It was a busy day, of course, and I rushed through what I was doing and dashed over to the bookshop fully aware that I would have only a few minutes there before I needed to be going somewhere else. Heading for the travel section I bumped — literally — into a friend I hadn't seen for at least three months. He was in a hurry too, and we proceeded to have a hasty conversation without even looking at one another as we both frantically scanned the bookshelves. It must have looked highly comical — two talking heads bobbing up and down the aisle. Finally we each grabbed a book, raced to the cash register and hollered good-bye as we sped off in opposite directions. Walking away, I felt suddenly flat, anticipation of a pleasurable pastime giving way to dulled disappointment. I had not enjoyed a meaningful conversation with my friend nor experienced the joy of browsing, and now I was carrying home a $12.50 book about London in the 1890s that I wasn't even sure I wanted.

Experiences like this are making me question the wisdom of zooming through each day. A full-throttle life seems to yield little satisfaction other than the sensation of speed itself. I've begun voicing these doubts to friends and have discovered that many of them share my dis-ease. But it's still a tricky topic to bring up in public. Speaking out against speed can get you lumped in with the Flat Earth Society as a hopelessly wrongheaded romantic who refuses to face the facts of modern life. Yet it's clear that more and more Americans desperately want to slow down. A surprising number of people I know have cut back to part-time jobs or quit altogether in order to work for themselves, raise kids, go back to school or find some other way to lead a more meaningful, less hurried life — even though it means getting by on significantly less income.

And according to Harvard economist Juliet Schor, these are not isolated cases. Author of the 1991 best-seller *The Overworked American*, Schor says her research shows that "millions of Americans are beginning to live a different kind of life, where they are trading money for time. I believe that this is one of the most important trends going on in America." Fed up with what compressed schedules are doing to their lives, many Americans want to move out of the fast lane; 28 percent in one study said that they have recently made voluntary changes that resulted in earning less money. These people tend to be more highly educated and younger than the US workforce as a whole, although they are being joined by other people who are involuntarily trading paychecks for time off through layoffs and under-employment.

People want to slow down because they feel that their lives are spinning out of control, which is ironic because speed has always been promoted as a way to help us achieve mastery over the world. "The major cause in the speed-up of life is not technology, but economics," says Schor. "The nature of work has changed now that bosses are demanding longer hours of work." After a long workweek, the rest of our life becomes a rat race, during which we have little choice but to hurry from activity to activity, with one eye always on the clock. Home-cooked meals give way to frozen pizzas, and Sundays turn into a hectic whirlwind of errands.

Yet there is a small but growing chorus of social critics, Schor among them, who dare to say that faster is not always better and that we must pay attention to the psychological, environmental and political consequences of our constantly accelerating world. Environmental activist Jeremy Rifkin was one of the first to raise questions about the desirability of speed in his 1987 book *Time Wars*.

> We have quickened the pace of life only to become less patient. We have become more organized but less spontaneous, less joyful. We are better prepared to act on the future but less able to enjoy the present and reflect on the past.
>
> As the tempo of modern life has continued to accelerate, we have come to feel increasingly out of touch with the biological rhythms of the planet, unable to experience a close connection with the natural environment. The human time world is no longer joined to the incoming and outgoing tides, the rising and setting sun, and the changing seasons. Instead, humanity has created an artificial time environment punctuated by mechanical contrivances and electronic impulses.

Rifkin closed his book with an eloquent call for a new social movement to improve the quality of life and defend the environment, a movement of people from all walks of life gathering under the "Slow Is Beautiful" banner. Perhaps appropriately, progress in forging such a movement has moved forward very slowly in the decade since *Time Wars* was published, while the pace of modern life has revved up considerably, thanks to breakthroughs in technology and new economic demands imposed by the globalizing economy.

Is Slow Really Beautiful?

The prominent German environmental thinker Wolfgang Sachs shares Hillis's interest in devising an aesthetic of slowness and offers his own ideas about what form it would take. "Medium speeds will be considered an accomplishment, something well done," he says. "And when you see someone going fast, you shrug your shoulders, saying, 'What's the point?'"

Sachs believes that speed is an under-recognized factor fueling environmental problems. As he puts it, "It's possible to talk about the ecological crisis as a collision between time scales — the fast time scale of modernity crashing up against the slow time scale of nature and the earth." In his view, genetic engineering, with all its potential for ecological havoc, is an example of how we interfere with natural processes in the name of speeding up evolution. Sachs's recent report *Sustainable Germany* — which maps a route to a green society — embraces slowing down as a key environmental objective, proposing to put 100-kilometer-an-hour speed limits on Germany's autobahns and scrap plans for a high-speed rail network. He also recommends strengthening local economies and cultures so that people won't have to rely as heavily on long-distance travel.

"A society that lives in the fast lane can never be a sustainable society," Sachs said in his report. "In a fast-paced world we put a lot of energy into arrivals and departures and less into the experience itself. Raising kids, making friends, creating art all run counter to the demand for speed. There is growing recognition that faster speeds are not just a natural fact of the universe. It's an issue for public attention. What has not been discussed before now is: What kind of speed do we want?"

Jogi Panghaal, a designer who works with community groups in India, defines the issue as not simply whether speed is good or bad, but whether the world of the future will allow a variety of speeds. He worries that a monoculture of speed in which the whole world is expected to move at the same pace will develop globally.

Sachs and Panghaal raise the question of whether we will have any choice in determining the tempo of our lives, or whether we'll all be dragged along by the furious push of a technologically charged society. When I hear friends complain that their lives move too fast, they're not talking about a wholesale rejection of speed so much as a wish that they could spend more of their time involved in slow, contemplative activities. One can love the revved-up beat of dance music, the fast-breaking action on the basketball court or the thrill of roller-coaster rides without wanting to live one's life at that pace. A balanced life, with intervals of creative frenzy giving way to relaxed tranquility, is what people crave. Yet the pressures of work, the demands of technology and the expectations of a fast-action society make this goal increasingly difficult to achieve.

Ezio Manzini, director of the Domus Academy design institute in Milan, sees hope for a more balanced approach to speed springing from the same source that fuels the acceleration of our lives: modern mastery of all that stands in our way. "This is the first time in history in which people think they can design their lives," he said.

In an age of technological marvels, we've come to expect that solutions will be found to help us overcome our problems. So if the problem now appears to be too many things coming at us too fast, we'll naturally begin looking for ways to slow down. Humans may not have opted for slowness in the past, but they have also never had to contend with constantly soaring speeds that not only diminish the quality of life, but also endanger the future of the planet.

How to Hasten Slowly

All these ideas are fine, but how do we even think about the enormous undertaking of slowing down a world that's been on a spiral of growing acceleration for more than a century and a half? Especially when the captains of the global economy dictate that speed is an essential ingredient of tomorrow's prosperity? How do we begin to apply the brakes in our lives when the world around us seems to be stomping on the gas pedal?

The city of Amsterdam itself seemed to offer an answer. More than almost any city in the world, Amsterdam has consciously curtailed the speed of traffic, creating a delightful urban environment in which a bike rolling past at 15 miles an hour seems speedy. Strolling the narrow streets for just a few minutes, you encounter all sorts of shops, restaurants, nightclubs, parks, public squares, banks and movie theaters — an impressive array of shopping and entertainment that would take at least an hour's worth of driving and parking to reach in most American cities. You're moving slower than in a car but experiencing much more.

Amsterdam's efforts have been widely imitated around the world by advocates of traffic calming, a burgeoning popular movement that seeks to improve safety and environmental quality by reducing the speed of cars. The spread of traffic-calming techniques like speed bumps throughout

Europe, Australia and now North America provides a sterling example of how a grassroots movement can bring about the slowing down of society.

This idea of calming could be taken out of the streets and into workplaces, government and civic organizations. It's true that transnational corporations wield near autocratic authority in today's global economy, but a spirited worldwide campaign for shorter work hours, more vacation and a less intense work pace might crystallize worker discontent into a potent political force that would undermine that power. Juliet Schor contends that additional leisure time, not further economic growth, will be the chief political goal of the coming age. (We've already seen the start, with women's groups and labor unions leading a successful campaign for family leave policies in American workplaces.)

But before any political movement can take hold, people need to begin thinking differently about speed and how important it really is. For 150 years we've been told (and believed) that the future will inevitably be faster than the present and that this is the best way to broaden human happiness. And speed has brought major improvements to our world. But in taking advantage of its possibilities, we have become blind to its drawbacks. While the acceleration of life that started with the first steam locomotive didn't crush our bones, it may have crushed our spirits. Our lives have grown so hurried and so hectic that we often don't take in the thrill of a sunset, the amusement of watching a youngster toddle down the sidewalk or the good fortune of bumping into a friend at a bookstore. We can regain the joy of those things without giving up the World Wide Web, ambulance service and airline flights to Amsterdam. Rather than accept that the world offers just one speed, we have the privilege, as Ezio Manzini says, of "designing" our lives.

Wolfgang Sachs, project director of the Wuppertal Institute for Climate, Energy, and the Environment in Wuppertal, Germany, says, "It's a struggle for me to slow down, as it is with many people. But the key is to be able to dedicate yourself to the proper rhythm, geared to what you are doing, whether you are playing with a child, writing a paper or talking to friends." One thing that keeps his life from whirling out of control is walking to work each day. Those strolls offer him 20 minutes each morning and evening when he's out of reach of the rushing insistence of the modern world.

Juliet Schor has slowed the pace of her life by setting firm limits on when she works. "My work time is limited by my childcare hours. I don't work on weekends. My life outside of work has also been simplified. I rarely drive a car. I ride my bike. I just don't do all the things that make me crazy. And my husband, who is from India and has a much calmer approach to life, has been instrumental in helping me slow down. He has taught me to just do one thing at a time."

We all have a chance to slow down. Maybe not at work or in raising kids, but someplace in our lives. It might be turning off the rapid-fire imagery of television and taking a stroll through the neighborhood. It might be scaling back the household budget and spending Saturdays fishing or gardening instead of shopping. It might be clearing a spot on your daily calendar for meditation, prayer or just daydreaming. It might be simply deciding to do less and not squeezing in a trip to the bookstore when you don't have time for a relaxing visit.

That's how I've started the "Slow Is Beautiful" revolution in my own life — right in the kitchen, scaling back my busy schedule to find more time for cooking good meals and then sitting down to enjoy them in a festive, unrushed way with my wife, son and friends. Even cleaning up after dinner can offer a lesson in the pleasures of slowness, as I learned a while back when our dishwasher went on the fritz. Before that, I had always just tossed dirty dishes into the machine as fast as possible and hurriedly wiped the counters so that I could get on to more worthwhile activities. But when I was forced to wash dishes by hand, I discovered that although it took longer I had way more fun; I'd put some jazz or blues on the stereo and sing along, or just daydream as I stacked dishes and glasses on the drying rack. What had been 5 or 10 minutes of drudgery, filling the dishwasher and desperately wishing I was doing something else, turned into 15 or 20 minutes of relaxation. Our dishwasher is fixed now, but I still find myself looking forward to cleaning up the kitchen. A lot of nights, I wash the dishes by hand anyway, and when I load the dishwasher, now I do it slowly and without the slightest hint of displeasure.

Creating the Educational Foundations for Change

by John E. Wear, Jr.

JOHN E. WEAR, JR. is an associate professor of biology and environmental science and founding director of the Center for the Environment at Catawba College, in Salisbury, North Carolina. He shows what colleges and universities can do about sustainability by working with both their campuses and communities. He has worked in many areas of sustainability: air and water quality, land conservation, wildlife, green buildings and community development.

John, a fellow of the American Leadership Forum, was named the 2003 North Carolina Conservationist of the Year by the Governor's Conservation Achievement Awards Program; a 2002 "Guardian of the Earth" by the *Charlotte Observer*; and the 2001 Green Builder of the Year by the Carolina Recycling Association.

SMALL WAVES LAPPED AGAINST our wooden flat-bottomed boat, occasionally spraying water onto baskets laden with vegetables and eggs. As we pulled up to his pier, Mr. Earle, who had seen us coming, walked down the hill from his cabin, eagerly anticipating the delivery of fresh produce for his evening meal. My sister, Susan, then 13, did the negotiating. At 11, I was her shy junior partner.

My job was to steer the three-horsepower motorboat and load the vegetables into bags for her to weigh and price. When the transaction was complete, we shoved off onto High Rock Lake and headed for our next customer, next pier over.

Early that morning, we had helped Dad pick vegetables and gather eggs for our fledgling floating enterprise. Our little farm — our family's summer retreat 20 minutes from our home in Salisbury, North Carolina — was perched on a hilltop. The rustic cabin, which had been on that site for more than 200 years, sat humbly under a magnificent oak with giant limbs that cast protective shadows over much of the yard. Bordering the yard on two sides was Dad's vegetable garden: tomatoes, zucchini, yellow squash, green beans, corn, watermelon; you name it, we grew it. That year, the yield was so abundant that my sister and I were able to earn extra spending money selling the excess — a practice we continued for several summers until my sister's interests turned elsewhere. In fact, there was no "nature deficit disorder" for me growing up in 1950s and '60s. My sister, two brothers and I were sent outdoors not only to work but to play, to collect our thoughts, to recover from that rare conflict with parents or siblings, or trouble in school; often, we went outside on our own just to sort things out and commune with nature.

As I grew into my teens, my father (who was a physician), my brother Ralph and I decided to try our hand at farming ventures; together we raised crops of corn and soybeans and developed a livestock operation that grew to 75 head of cattle and five breeds of horses. In so doing, we connected with neighboring farmers with whom we shared equipment, labor and expertise. We pitched in, in a spirit of good will and reciprocity, to help as they needed us, knowing they'd gladly return the favor.

These rural experiences cemented my understanding of humanity's deep connection to and dependence on nature. I can see now, decades later, that those formative early years created in me a deep reverence for the land, for nature and for our role as stewards of this Earth. As recent research has demonstrated, lacking a connection to nature is damaging to the development of the young as well as to the quality of life of us all.

Experiential Learning

My early connection with the natural world helped direct me to a life devoted to educating others about the environment. It laid the foundation for my core beliefs. Those early experiences ultimately brought me back to Salisbury in 1993 to start up the environmental program at Catawba College. That initiative spawned the creation of the Catawba College Center for the Environment in 1996, which is committed to educating both students and the general public about environmental stewardship and sustainability and to involving the faculty, staff, students and Center partners in programs and activities in our community and region. Concurrently, the environmental science and studies program was developed to provide students with a multidisciplinary education in fields of study related to the environment. We seek to foster in our students the spirit of teamwork and service, in addition to academic study.

The surprisingly outsized initial (and continuing) interest in this field led to the construction of our home facility, a signature green building that now serves as the fulcrum for much campus and community activity. This three-story building — also called Catawba College Center for the Environment — houses classrooms, larger conference and multipurpose rooms, a library and offices. The Center is a place where much environmental learning takes place but is also the welcome mat to our community.

Completed in 2001 — and planned prior to the acceptance of LEED-certification standards — the center is a green building that used recycled and recyclable materials, as well as sustainably harvested timber and grasses like bamboo. A geo-exchange system was installed to heat and cool the 21,000-square-foot facility. The building was positioned to exploit the natural sunlight, and large overhangs were placed to mitigate the effects of the summer sun. Solar panels on the roof generate energy used in the building and also to juice an electric vehicle for the center's adjacent 189-acre nature preserve. Thoughtful touches abound throughout the compound, including an 80-foot stretch of permeable pavement to absorb rainwater; a collection cistern fills the many ponds that surround the building's naturalistic landscaping.

Working along with other faculty and departments on campus, our goal is to provide students with experiential learning in nature while maintaining a keen focus on environmental issues. We seek to provide students with experiences beyond those that a small liberal arts college of around 1,200 students might normally provide. There are currently four different environmental degree programs: environmental science; environmental studies; environmental education; and sustainable business and community development.

Outside the normal curriculum, we work to involve and empower students, giving them large responsibilities, such as making recommendations to the college trustees that come out of our Campus Greening course. Among the student recommendations that have been implemented was the creation of a waste management and recycling office that now operates under the campus's facilities department. As an extension of that initiative, the program is now

targeting the composting of food waste at all campus caf-
eterias. Energy conservation measures and a campus-wide
recycling program are also in place — largely due to earlier
student-led initiatives.

Reaching out to the Community

A cornerstone of the Center's mission — and what sets us
apart from other environmental education programs around
the nation — has long been our work to educate citizens of
the region, alongside Catawba's undergraduates. We work
to connect with — and empower — a diverse population
not only in Rowan County, of which Salisbury is the county
seat, but also in a 13-county area extending from Charlotte
to Winston-Salem, North Carolina. Given the large number
of attendees in our programs through the years, we know
that significant ownership exists in the community for our
work. Shifting people's mindsets — especially in this traditionally conservative section of the Southeast — so that
they consider walking more lightly on the Earth has been
no simple task. But we can proudly point to numerous vic-
tories that underscore missions accomplished.

To serve as a catalyst for change, the Center hosts speaking events, symposia and conferences eight to ten times
yearly. Outside guest experts are brought in to help spear-
head conversations about issues in which we'd like to engage
the community. Our work has been to not only educate but
to act as a catalyst. For example, amidst a backdrop of a set of
county commissioners opposed to any form of countywide
planning, back in 2006, we brought in Randall Arendt, the
author and expert in conservation planning and development, to lend his expertise and leadership. His innovative
development plans are considered "twice green" because
they succeed in both environmental and economic terms.
Arendt gave a one-day workshop that was well attended

by community planners and leaders from the region. A shorter evening program attracted mostly members of the Salisbury community. Two years after his presentation, one of the county commissioners who'd been most vocally opposed to the concept was presented with a plan that might as well have been taken directly from Arendt's playbook. This commissioner was quoted as saying, "I love this concept — conservation development."

Likewise, I have worked long and hard to build a bridge to the business community, including developers, to offer our educational resources to their changing industry. I've found that while some building contractors and developers wouldn't make time for workshops, they would accept an invitation for dinner at a first-class restaurant where we could break bread and talk turkey. One of the realizations that came out of one such bank-sponsored four-course meal was that a lot of developers were interested in going green but bureaucratic red tape was holding them back. Out of that seminal dinner, we developed a roundtable committee of city planners and developers to work out difficulties they were having in getting new plans approved. What I learned from this experience is that each new issue that comes up requires formulating a new game plan to bring others on board.

Though Americans often clamor for quick results, over 16 years of work with the Center, we've learned that seeds planted may not bear immediate fruit. But give these issues time to develop, cultivate friendships and relationships — even with those who may express opposition — and you may be pleased and delighted with eventual results.

One of the Center's earliest initiatives and success stories in acting as a change agent in our community was a partnership with the city of Salisbury to create a greenway program.

Our strategy was to create a linear park for recreation, alternative transportation and nature observation surrounding the city (some of which extends through the campus). We created a committee and spent the first five years making the project a reality, through gaining access rights and raising our own grant money before asking the city for funding. Strategically, we recognized correctly that if we first made the greenway a reality, we might fly under the radar screens of the naysayers. Once the greenway was in place, we figured, the benefits would speak for themselves, and no one would want to dismantle this amazing green asset.

Another example of a successful Center initiative was organizing a study to demonstrate the true value of tree resources in the community. To do this, we brought together organizations and people who could successfully create an ongoing satellite study that now benefits communities throughout our region. The study was able to attach a monetary value to the tree canopy, thus quantifying the real value of our tree resources for business leaders and others. This undertaking is linked closely with another key Center outreach program, our ongoing Clean Air Initiative.

The world has changed a great deal during the 200 years since my family's cabin was built. The technological world we now live in separates us from the quiet rural life that allowed our internal voice to speak to us and tell us to care for creation. The technological complexity, the sights, sounds and distractions of the world drown out that simple message. Yet we need it now more than ever.

With the compounding issues related to population, food, energy, water and increasing levels of pollutants in the environment, the next 25 years will be exceedingly challenging. Change in the way we live on this Earth will be necessary, and that change will need to take place at a rate that exceeds the rate at which this planet is being degraded.

Catalysts for Change

Centers like ours serve as a catalyst for positive change. We play a vital role in guiding our communities in their efforts to lessen their footprint. By assuming a non-confrontational stance, by working in partnership with members of the community, we help students and citizens alike cope with a world where things that were once predictable no longer are, where environmental degradation affects everyone's life. A center can help members of a community see trends and make connections and look beyond the issues to discover the root causes.

Our Center does not advocate for specific issues but instead encourages a community shift to greater awareness and action. In this way, we are able to reach the greatest number of people. We function as a portal allowing involvement by people not traditionally involved with environmental issues. In order to be that portal, we have to do several things. First, we have to speak in a language that focuses on our commonalities; second, we need to show people the connections between their actions and the impact those actions have on the world around them; and finally, we need to create the tools they need to make the changes we hope they will make.

To encourage people to steward the Earth, it is important to remember that individuals do not start their journey at the same place. As I was blessed from my earliest years, some people are more connected to the natural world; some have had the rich experiences that tie us to our Earth and lay the foundation for our spirituality. Others have not been as fortunate.

A Simple Message

So how can we talk to people with diverse worldviews and get them to follow a simple message, a message that we need to walk more lightly on this Earth? How do we get those who are different from us, sometimes radically different, to shift their thinking and become part of this greater movement?

The message we receive through those quiet, contemplative relationships with the natural world is a message that is put together slowly: We realize that each component in the natural world fits together, piece by piece, much like the pieces of a puzzle. It is a message that tells us that within the workings of all ecosystems on our planet are the clues for how we are to live on this Earth. Some complete the puzzle and receive the message. Others are still on the path. I wish all young people today were blessed as I was with a wealth of experiences connecting them viscerally to the natural world. We must reach out to those whose worldview differs from ours. We must meet them where they are and help them see how all the pieces fit together, how living lightly on the Earth is our only viable choice.

PART THREE

Policies

Introduction

by Cecile Andrews

IN SOCIAL CHANGE CIRCLES, there's often a debate about which is more important: individual changes or policy changes. But the debate is irrelevant. We need both. Without policy changes, there will be no real change. For instance, unless we establish a policy, as they do in Europe, that everyone is entitled to four weeks vacation, there will always be some businesses that give only one or two (or none), hoping this will make them more competitive.

So policies are crucial. But there will be no policies without individual change because that's what creates a movement. We need a movement to press the government for policy change. For instance, when women made individual changes in their lives, they themselves were changed. They became feminists and worked for the rights of women.

Thus, we need both individual change and policy change, but the American public, with its culture of rugged individualism, is slow to understand this. We still have an anti-government bias, but now we're being forced to re-examine this as we struggle to create a healthy economy.

One thing is clear. Whenever we have allowed corporations to be unregulated, whenever we have allowed the pursuit of profit at any price, whenever we have put too much power into the hands of the few, the economy has gone bad. Our economic policies must support the greater good for the greater number. Otherwise, the unchecked pursuit of profit will continue to destroy the planet and its people.

Most of the contributors to this book have, to some extent, discussed policies needed to address the issues of economic crisis, climate change and personal happiness. I think of this effort as building a culture of Simplicity — where *everyone* can live more simply: consume less, work less and have time for the important things in life. In particular, we need specific policies for things like shorter work hours, a smaller wealth gap and a green economy. We need policies to encourage — rather than discourage — caring for the common good.

We need policies that change people's behavior so that they change their belief systems: For instance, people will only care about the common good when government policies guarantee equality — otherwise, everyone just wants policies that benefit themselves. Allowing people to pursue profit without principle or letting corporations go unregulated will create a cutthroat society and destroy equality and caring.

The policies that our authors write about are tremendously important, and getting involved in pressuring our government to pass these policies is one of the most satisfying things a person can do. Ultimately, working toward such policies helps people feel they have more power, more integrity and more self-worth — all qualities that undermine consumerism. The person with self-respect has no desire to hang out at a mall.

Ultimately, all change is linked. I love the story from FDR, when a group of citizens came to him with an idea, and he said, "I agree with you; now go out and force me to do it."

A Mature Economy

by Bill McKibben

BILL MCKIBBEN is an American environmentalist and
writer who frequently writes about global warming, alternative energy and the risks associated with human
genetic engineering. Beginning in the summer of 2006,
he led the organization of the largest demonstrations
against global warming in American history. Beginning
in January 2007, Bill founded StepItUp2007.org to demand that Congress enact curbs on carbon emissions
that would cut global warming pollution 80 percent by
2050. His books include *Hope, Human and Wild* and
*Deep Economy: The Wealth of Communities and the Du-
rable Future.*

IF THERE WAS ever an idea that won widespread support, it
was the notion of economic growth. Oddly, though, given
the way it's taken over the world, the notion of infinite economic expansion is fairly new. During the Depression, for
instance, even FDR routinely spoke of America's economy
as mature, with no further expansion anticipated. We had
too many factories, he said — we were making everything
we could possibly need and then some. Hoover argued
the opposite — scientists had thousands of inventions just
waiting for the capital that would set them free. And though
Hoover lost the election, he won the battle — he was in fact
the better prophet.

That was obvious by the end of World War II and the boom that followed — we were clearly on the edge of a new kind of mass prosperity. By the time Lyndon Johnson moved into the White House in 1963, he said things like: "I'm sick of all the people who talk about the things we can't do. Hell, we're the richest country in the world, the most powerful. We can do it all.... We can do it if we believe it." He wasn't alone in thinking this way. From Moscow, Nikita Khrushchev thundered, "Growth of industrial and agricultural production is the battering ram with which we shall smash the capitalist system."

Yet even then, the bad news was already apparent, if you cared to look. Burning rivers and smoggy cities demonstrated the dark side of industrial expansion. In 1972, a trio of MIT researchers released a series of computer forecasts they called "Limits to Growth," which showed that unbridled expansion would eventually deplete our resource base. A year later, the British economist E. F. Schumacher wrote the best-selling *Small Is Beautiful*. By 1979, the sociologist Amitai Etzioni reported to President Carter that only 30 percent of Americans were "pro-growth," 31 percent were "anti-growth," and 39 percent were "highly uncertain."

Such ambivalence, Etzioni predicted, "is too stressful for societies to endure," and Ronald Reagan proved his point. He convinced us it was "Morning in America" — out with limits, in with Trump. Today, mainstream liberals and conservatives compete mainly on the question of who can flog the economy harder. Larry Summers, who served as Bill Clinton's secretary of the treasury, at one point declared that the Clinton administration "cannot and will not accept any 'speed limit' on American economic growth. It is the task of economic policy to grow the economy as rapidly, sustainably, and inclusively as possible." It's the economy, stupid.

Except there are three small things. The first I'll mention

mostly in passing: Even though the economy continues to grow, most of us are no longer getting wealthier. The average wage in the United States is less now, in real dollars, than it was 30 years ago. Even for those with college degrees, and although productivity was growing faster than it had for decades, between 2000 and 2004, earnings fell 5.2 percent when adjusted for inflation, according to the most recent data from White House economists. Much the same thing has happened across most of the globe. More than 60 countries, in fact, have seen income per capita fall in the past decade.

For the second trouble, just look at the price on the gas pump. It's been heading north because we're running short of oil — and oil is the commodity that has made economic growth possible. It has provided us with a battalion of slaves that has made life completely different. Economists have trouble realizing this; their standard idea is that if we run short of something, it will pay for someone to develop a substitute. In general this has proved true in the past: Run short of nice big sawlogs, and someone invents plywood. But it's far from clear that the same precept applies to coal, oil and natural gas. This time, there is no easy substitute: I like the solar panels on my roof, but they're collecting diffuse daily energy, not using up eons of accumulated power. Fossil fuel was an exception to the rule, a one-time gift that underwrote a one-time binge of growth.

This brings us to the third point: If we do try to keep going, with the entire world aiming for an economy structured like America's, it won't be just oil that we'll run short of. Here are the numbers we have to contend with: Given current rates of growth in the Chinese economy, the 1.3 billion residents of that nation alone will, by 2031, be about as rich as we are. If they then eat meat, milk and eggs at the rate that we do, calculates eco-statistician Lester Brown,

they will consume 1,352 million tons of grain each year —
equal to two-thirds of the world's entire 2004 grain harvest.
They will use 99 million barrels of oil a day, 15 million more
than the entire world consumes at present. They will use
more steel than all the West combined, double the world's
production of paper and drive 1.1 billion cars — 1.5 times as
many as the current world total. And that's just China; by
then, India will have a bigger population, and its economy
is growing almost as fast. And then there's the rest of the
world.

It's hard for the political system, or the economics profession, to deal with these kinds of reality. That's because
they are entirely convinced that more is the point — that
growing the amount of stuff is the same as growing the
amount of happiness. But in the last few years, some of the
more adventurous researchers have begun to realize that the
world is more complicated than they knew. They've begun
to do something strange for economics — they've begun to
count in twos and threes, not ones. They've begun to understand community.

Traditional economists think of human beings primarily as individuals and not as members of a community, and
therefore, it turns out, they miss out on a major part of
what actually satisfies us. But the data is getting so strong
that you can lay it out as a mathematical equation. Overall,
"evidence shows that companionship…contributes more to
well-being than does income," writes Robert E. Lane, a Yale
political science professor who wrote *The Loss of Happiness
in Market Democracies*. But there is a notable difference between poor and wealthy countries: When people have lots of
companionship but not much money, income "makes more
of a contribution to subjective well-being." By contrast,
"where money is relatively plentiful and companionship
relatively scarce, companionship will add more to subjec-

tive well-being." If you are a poor person in China, you have plenty of friends and family around all the time — perhaps there are four other people living in your room. Adding a sixth doesn't make you happier. But adding enough money so that all five of you can eat some meat from time to time pleases you greatly. By contrast, if you live in a suburban American home, buying another coffeemaker adds very little to your quantity of happiness — trying to figure out where to store it, or wondering if you picked the perfect model, may in fact decrease your total pleasure. But a new friend, a new connection, is a big deal. We have a surplus of individualism and a deficit of companionship, and so the second becomes more valuable.

Indeed, we seem to be genetically wired for community. As biologist Edward O. Wilson found, most primates live in groups and get sad when they're separated: "an isolated individual will repeatedly pull a lever with no reward other than the glimpse of another monkey." Why do people so often look back on their college days as the best years of their lives? Because their classes were so fascinating? Or because in college we live more closely and intensely with a community than most of us ever do before or after? Every measure of psychological health points to the same conclusion: People who "are married, who have good friends, and who are close to their families are happier than those who do not," says Swarthmore psychologist Barry Schwartz. "People who participate in religious communities are happier than those who do not." Which is striking, Schwartz adds, because social ties "actually decrease freedom of choice" — being a good friend involves sacrifice.

Do we just think we're happier in communities? Is it merely some sentimental good-night-John-Boy affectation? No — our bodies react in measurable ways. According to research cited by Harvard professor Robert Putnam in his classic book, *Bowling Alone*, if you do not belong to any group at present, joining a club or a society of some kind cuts in half the risk that you will die in the next year. Check this out: When researchers at Carnegie Mellon (somewhat disgustingly) dropped samples of cold virus directly into subjects' nostrils, those with rich social networks were four times less likely to get sick. An economy that produces only individualism undermines us in the most basic ways.

Here's another statistic worth keeping in mind: Consumers have ten times as many conversations at farmers' markets as they do at supermarkets — an order of magnitude difference. By itself, that's hardly life-changing, but it points at something that could be: living in an economy where you are participant as well as consumer, where you have a sense of who's in your universe and how it all fits together. At the same time, some studies show local agriculture using less energy (also by an order of magnitude) than the "it's always summer somewhere" system we operate on now. Those are big numbers, and it's worth thinking about what they suggest — especially since, between peak oil and climate change, there's no longer really a question that we'll have to wean ourselves of the current model.

So as a mental experiment, imagine how we might shift to a more sustainable kind of economy. You could use government policy to nudge the change — remove subsidies from agribusiness and use them instead to promote farmer-entrepreneurs; underwrite the cost of windmills with even a fraction of the money that's now going to protect oil flows. You could put tariffs on goods that travel long distances, shift highway spending to projects that make it easier to live near where you work (and, by cutting down on commutes, leave some time to see the kids).

It's easy to dismiss such ideas as sentimental or nostalgic. In fact, economies can be localized as easily in cities and suburbs as rural villages (maybe more easily) and in ways that look as much to the future as the past, which rely more on the solar panel and the Internet than the white picket fence. In fact, given the trendlines for phenomena such as global warming and oil supply, what's nostalgic and sentimental is to keep doing what we're doing simply because it's familiar.

Why Isn't This Empire Sustainable?

by David Wann

DAVID WANN is the co-author of the best-seller *Affluenza* and author of *Simple Prosperity: Finding Real Wealth in a Sustainable Lifestyle*. To find out more, visit Dave online at DaveWann.com.

IF SO MANY ARE WILLING to die for our country, why are we afraid to *live* for it, moderately and unselfishly? Why do we place a higher value on convenience, size and speed than the well-being of living things (including ourselves)? The many globally scaled challenges we now face will require major social and psychological adjustments, not just new technologies. We need to change the *patterns* of our lives (where we live, how we work, what we eat), not just the pieces. Yet, cultural inertia and consumer euphoria perpetuate an unrealistic hope that our familiar way of life can continue without significant changes. If we just screw in some compact fluorescent bulbs and remember to take cloth bags to the grocery, maybe we can avoid the need to rethink our relationship with the Earth? The wishful assumption is that once we bring new technologies on line — such as plug-in hybrid vehicles, super-efficient buildings and huge wind farms — we're there, right?

Not exactly. Certainly, these simple habit changes and brilliant technologies are critical, urgently needed pieces of an emerging Restoration Economy, but they are not sufficient. Until we change the *direction* of our plug-and-play lifestyle, we'll continue to be an endangered as well as dangerous civilization. We'll continue to generate high levels of carbon dioxide as we plunder rich, climax ecosystems for the sake of must-have gadgets and nutrition-free, processed food.

We can't change the realities of resource scarcity and natural limits, so we must change ourselves instead. Consumer cultures like ours urgently need value-directed policies that reward efficiency and durability and penalize overconsumption. Too often, we don't issue guidelines bold enough to break bad habits. For example, between 1980 and 1990, mandated upgrades in automobile efficiency held transportation's share of oil consumption steady; but the pampered American psyche demanded larger and more powerful vehicles, erasing the efficiency gains and increasing oil demand, a major factor in rising gasoline prices.

Similarly, household appliances steadily became more efficient, but those gains were literally overpowered when huge-screen TVs, computers and Play Stations began to define what we do indoors. Electrical consumption in the average household is climbing beyond the capacity of roof-mounted solar electric systems, an otherwise very promising technology. The fact is, renewable energies like solar, wind and geothermal *can* meet the needs of a moderate, no-waste economy, but not a careless, hyper-consumptive economy.

Since 1950, the average American home doubled in size, miles traveled per capita (on the road and in the air) more than tripled, and US per capita consumption of energy-intensive meat more than doubled. Since 1975, US consumption of plastic-bottled water skyrocketed more than 2,000 percent, as Americans pursued a false symbol of health, stylishness and purity. We can't become truly sustainable until we curb our appetites for energy hogs like throwaway packaging, expansive green lawns, suburbs without stores and air-freighted produce. Simply finding substitutes for today's fuels and technologies won't break the ongoing fever of overproduction and overconsumption.

Only by rethinking and redefining words like "enough" and "success" can we steer our society in a sunnier direction. Congressman Dennis Kucinich recently suggested that status — a universal human need — should be based on *service*, not consumption. Adopting this suggestion as an unselfish social goal could change the very nature of the economic game we are so destructively playing.

In the emerging, more mindful economy, we'll be better attuned to what nature needs, and what it can supply. For example, one of the most effective ways to counter global warming is to plant millions of trees, yet many tree-planting efforts have faltered because the planters failed to nurture the trees to maturity. Our busy schedules don't leave time for learning about nature, yet it's the busy schedules that must change, because if we continue to perceive nature as just an ornamental backdrop and warehouse of raw materials, our legacy will be a holocaust of barren, lifeless habitats.

Our ideal destination, a sustainable culture that delivers more satisfaction for fewer resources, will require slowing the metabolism of human civilization itself, for example, by improving the usefulness — sometimes questioning the very necessity — of manufactured goods. The overall goal is to produce goods and services the way bees produce honey, without harming the flower

Historian Arnold Toynbee observed that civilizations that ultimately succeed follow a "law of progressive simplification," in which they become culturally richer but materially leaner. America is poised to make such an elegant transition under new leadership, as countries like Costa Rica and Denmark already have. In a sustainable economy, based not on *quantity* of life but quality of life, we'll consume fewer things but better things, reducing the total volume of transactions, the total throughput of materials and, in the process, increase our gladness to be alive.

Symptoms of a Declining Civilization

- Resource stocks fall, and wastes and pollution accumulate.
- Resources and capital are diverted to compensate for the loss of services formerly provided free by nature.
- Exploitation of scarcer, more distant, deeper or more dilute resources.
- Growing chaos in natural systems, with "natural" disasters more frequent.
- Growing demands for capital, resources and labor used by the military or industry to gain access to and defend resources.
- Investment in human resources (education, health care, shelter) postponed in order to meet immediate consumption or security needs, or to pay debts.
- Declining respect for the values of the public sector and true democracy.

[Adapted from Donnella H. Meadows, Dennis L. Meadows and Jørgen Randers, *Beyond the Limits: Confronting Global Collapse, Envisioning A Sustainable Future*, Chelsea Green, 1992.]

Yet, it's undeniable that the American way of life is designed for maximum consumption and "tolerable" amounts of environmental destruction. A few centuries ago, this seemed like a logical strategy, but we are now nearing peak consumption, and the only prudent pathway is down. When global population was only one-tenth as large as it is now and the world's resources seemed infinite, we structured an economy around extractive technologies, new individualistic freedoms and consumer spending. We created a cultural story in which anyone could amass material wealth if he or she was sufficiently industrious and persistent. The concept of economic growth became the dominant theme.

So ingrained is the story that we rarely question its implications. The reality is that the faster the global economy expands (well beyond "enough"), the faster the world's fragile living systems decline. Each American now requires an average of 30 acres of prime land and sea to satisfy both the needs and wants of our excessive lifestyle — a national total of roughly nine billion acres. Since this is more than three times the acreage of the United States, we'll have to bully other countries to continue our own absurd levels of consumption. We'll have to allocate more capital to the military, work even harder and longer at our jobs and carry a heavier burden of stress, debt, doubt and shame. We'll be ordered to react to crises like 9/11, Katrina and the housing meltdown with "patriotic," unnecessary shopping. That is, unless we decide, at last, to modify and moderate our story.

There are many other ways to measure and experience quality of life besides material wealth: time affluence, the joy and contentment of health, strong bonds with other people, civic participation, creativity, kindness, autonomy, security, serenity, generosity, wisdom and so on. Yet these forms of real wealth are often neglected as we chase from one job, errand or appointment to another, trying to buy what we could obtain far more directly if the story had a different plot and our system was set up differently. In recent polls (Gallup, CNN, Pew, etc.), more than half of all Americans say they would gladly trade a day's pay every week for an extra day off, but the official 40-hour workweek is a cardinal rule here. Meanwhile, in countries like Holland and Denmark, up to 40 percent of the population works part-time with no reduction in pay, protected by non-discrimination laws.

Two-thirds of Americans say they'd choose to live in a small town if possible, and a similar number would trade their trophy home for a mid-sized home in a great neighborhood, but there aren't enough small towns and great neighborhoods to go around. In fact, many zoning and building codes effectively make the design of walkable, diverse neighborhoods illegal, partly because they don't accommodate cars well enough or fit the "normal" pattern. But a new normal is emerging, very quickly. There's no doubt Americans want a different direction on environmental matters. For example, four out of five Americans now favor mandatory controls on greenhouse gas emissions; nine out of ten want higher auto fuel-efficiency standards; three out of four want clean electricity, even with slightly higher rates; and almost three out of four support more funding for mass transit.

Americans are tired of feeling passive and uncreative in our daily lives. Psychologist Mihaly Csikszentmihalyi's research describes a condition he calls "flow" in which the ego falls away and time flies by. After a flow experience, we are not only refreshed, but we've increased our skills and self-confidence. To be genuinely happy, we need to *actively* create our experiences and our lives, rather than passively letting media and marketers create them for us. Whether we experience it at work or in our off-hours, pursuing flow is a great antidote for affluenza, because if we are content in the moment, consumption loses its appeal.

We need more time for living, taking care of the children and rediscovering the flow in our lives, but our mainstream lifestyle drains time away. The typical American spends six months of his life sitting at red lights, eight months opening junk mail, one year searching for misplaced items, four years cleaning house, and five years waiting in line — all activities that relate to our lives as dutiful consumers. Only 14 percent of Americans will get a vacation of two weeks or longer this year, because, unlike 127 other countries, the US has no minimum paid-leave law. Though the Australians have four weeks off by law, the Europeans four and five weeks and the Japanese two weeks, our own record of "downtime" is abysmal.

From 1930 to 1985 (as productivity continued to soar per unit of labor), Kellogg company employees worked unique six-hour days, demonstrating real quality-of-life improvements. With ten hours more discretionary time each week, these employees helped transform the local lifestyle of Battle Creek, Michigan: families and neighborhoods became more lively, schools introduced curricula about the "arts of living," and parental involvement in schools — such as room mothers in classrooms — increased. Parks, community centers, skating rinks, churches and libraries became centers of activity. Kellogg workers recall that the balance of their lives shifted from working to living. What to do with their time became more important than what to buy with their money.

Social traits such as learned helplessness and naïve optimism prevent us from becoming sustainable, and so do policies that steer the market away from sustainability rather than toward efficiency, durability and recyclability. A few examples are subsidies to oil and gas companies but not renewable energy companies, agricultural subsidies that reward five target crops based on yield rather than sustainable farming, and sluggish fuel efficiency standards that reward the automobile and petroleum industries but punish American drivers.

If Americans want to live in a more sustainable, sensible and satisfying world, we need to steer our culture, economy and policies into a joyfully moderate new era.

Policies That Reward Sustainability

1. US income tax policy discourages saving and investing by taking a bite out of income. **Solution:** Lower income taxes and instead tax carbon-heavy fuels and technologies, as more than 20 European Union (EU) countries already have.
2. Mandatory 40-hour workweeks don't offer workers the choice of trading less income for more time. **Solution:** Enact laws that guarantee equal pay for part-time workers, as many EU countries already have.
3. The lack of a national healthcare policy (already in place in most industrial countries) necessitates work that is sometimes unwanted in order to retain health benefits. **Solution:** Implement universal health care and shift the US from a treatment to a preventive healthcare mentality.
4. Free parking at workplaces rewards driving but offers no incentives to pedestrians, bicyclers and carpoolers. **Solution:** Give a stipend to all employees, allowing non-drivers to save money if they choose.
5. Daycare tax credits assume that employees would rather pay for daycare than work less and care for their own children. **Solution:** Credit a fixed amount per US child; let parents choose how to spend it.
6. Flat-rate trash policies discourage recycling. **Solution:** Implement "pay as you throw" policies that penalize disposal and enable recyclers to save money.
7. Current beverage container policies don't reward recycling. **Solution:** Enact a federal "bottle bill" law, as 11 states already have.
8. Suburban sprawl wastes time, money, land and energy. **Solution:** Enact local, state and federal policies that encourage public transit and compact development.

Radical Sustainability

by Jim Merkel

JIM MERKEL wrote *Radical Simplicity* and has worked as the sustainability coordinator at Dartmouth College. The Exxon Valdez disaster and the invasion of Iraq prompted Jim, originally a military engineer trained in foreign military sales, to devote his life to Simplicity, social justice and world peace. He founded the Global Living Project (GLP) and initiated the GLP Summer Institute where teams of researchers attempted to live on an equitable portion of the biosphere.

THE FOREST IS STILL. Very still. In the distance, water flows over moss-covered boulders. A light drip hits the tent every so often. My aching body musters the strength to roll over in the twisted sleeping bag to check the time — 1:34 PM. After countless snooze-alarm cycles, waking to a steady downpour, I silence the alarm and release my plans to cover 12 more miles of the Appalachian Trail in favor of much-needed rest.

Yesterday's walk was otherworldly, breaking camp in the dark with a fat mist floating in the headlight's beam. The forecast called for severe thunderstorms and hail. I took my chances. I hoisted the 80-pound pack to a knee, braced in a squat, swung it while lacing my arm through the shoulder strap, then cinched the waist belt until it hurt. Wet sphagnum moss and bunchberries lined the trail as I worked my way up and over fogged-in summits. In the alpine, the stunted rhodora, Labrador tea and blueberry, all in bloom, heightened the sense of here and now.

I crossed Mt. Pierce, Eisenhower, Franklin and Monroe and made my way down to the Lakes of the Clouds as peek holes opened and revealed sweeping forest lungs, ravines and snakelike ridgelines. Mt. Washington stood ominous at 6,288 feet. As I began the ascent, it started to rain. I dropped my heavy pack and donned the rain gear as the clicks of hiking poles below gained steadily. It was the three college students I camped near last night. They were hiking under the trail names Hurricane, One-Flop and Stride. Their trip began 1,842 miles to the south, in Springer, Georgia. They, too, stopped to suit up. I peered at their tiny packs and wondered if one of them slipped their food into mine.

"Got a tent in there?" I asked.

"Yup," one of them said.

"A cookstove?"

"No."

"How much does that thing weigh?" I inquired.

"Twenty-five pounds."

Seeing "aching back" written across my face, they consoled me by saying they'd sent boxes of stuff home.

Most of my gear is 10 to 20 years old and fairly lightweight. It has crossed Canada twice by bike and been dragged all over British Columbia, the Himalayas, Mexico and New England. New ultralight gear would shave pounds, but it was the careless packing and unnecessary creature comforts that did me in. In other words, Simplicity (or lack thereof) could have trumped technology. For the next three weeks, I'd come out for food and send home another box of gear, getting down to 35 pounds by the last week while vowing to own a one-pound pack, tent and sleeping bag by the next trip.

I find it all too easy to slip out of Simplicity. When the excess is on your back, the feedback is immediate. Back home, integrating those boxes of excess gear back into my two-story, 14-by-16-foot cabin, everything felt excessive after weeks with only a single spoon as a utensil. Feedback at home had been subtle, like forcing another coat into the closet or another file into the cabinet. Other forms of feedback — such as the rising cost of food and fuel — motivate one to make better lists, shop by bike or expand the vegetable garden. And an odd form of feedback that shapes itself into a morning panic, lying in bed running over the to-do list — too many commitments, too many details, too many fun things to do and a mind unable to enjoy each waking moment.

In 1853, Henry David Thoreau said, "Simplify, simplify, simplify." Such repetition for a deliberate guy has to make you wonder. That mantra was, like his famous act of civil disobedience, a direct response to his neighbors' inability to say *"Enough"*. With all of our technological advances, with a population heading for 10 billion, with 1,000-fold species extinction rates and the scourge of climate change, with America's growing arsenal of weapons of mass destruction, with world poverty, food shortages and genetically modified organisms, Thoreau's mantra is proving more important than ever.

Much of my current work is on college campuses, where I consult, lecture and lead workshops on personal and institutional sustainability. When I was hired as Dartmouth College's Sustainability Coordinator in 2005, all other Ivy League campuses had sustainability positions, along with hundreds of other campuses. Dartmouth's energy bill had just increased from four to seven million dollars in one year, and it needed to save money and keep pace.

Across the nation, campuses are upgrading their buildings, reducing waste, purchasing wind or solar energy, changing investments, starting organic farms, integrating sustainability into campus culture, initiating new courses and degree programs and purchasing fair-trade, local and organic food. By fall 2008, 582 campuses had signed the American College and University Presidents Climate Commitment, agreeing to establish a date for becoming carbon neutral and completing a carbon inventory and reduction plan. Carbon neutral — that's right — means no net carbon emissions from campus operations. Now that's radical.

Is this even possible for campuses that have sizable infrastructures, high flows of inputs (water, electricity, energy, food, services) and outputs (greenhouse gases, air and water pollutants, solid and toxic wastes, biological wastes) and a culture of frequent local and global travel? Theoretically it is possible to get very close to carbon neutral, because a good percentage of the world's people do it everyday. Colleges, however, have a long way to go, and when they'll get there, if ever, is anyone's guess.

Let me share a sustainability strategy useful to individuals and institutions that can achieve or beat the popular call to reduce greenhouse gasses (GHG) by 80 percent by 2050.

The first step of this strategy is to identify as many independent factors that influence an institution's or individual's impact for a given activity. Let's start with a big-ticket item, the automobile. Independent factors include:

- How many people share the vehicle?
- How many miles per month are driven?
- How efficient is the vehicle?
- How long might this vehicle last?

Assume you drive alone, get 20 mpg and spend $160 to buy 40 gallons of gas each month. This translates into a four-acre footprint (forest area to sequester CO_2 from the tailpipe, manufacture and infrastructure). Then you get motivated by *An Inconvenient Truth*, the tragedy of a needless oil war and $4 per gallon gas. So you organize enough ride-sharing to average two people in your car. Determined to halve the miles traveled each month, you make detailed shopping lists, bike and walk more and prioritize visits to nearby friends. From the classifieds, you purchase a used 40-mpg vehicle. Without ecological heroics, you now buy five gallons of gas per month, use half an acre of ecological space and only spend $20.

But you're not done yet. You start a logbook for tire pressure, oil changes and maintenance. You drive slower and care for the vehicle enough to double its longevity, halving both its manufacture and disposal footprints. Because it's an older vehicle, you save money by removing collision from your insurance policy.

These advanced techniques of sharing, caring and conserving contribute to a phenomenon known as multiplication. Our example achieves the 80 percent reduction scientists like James Hansen say are necessary, at least for your car. I suspect readers will not wait until 2050 to experiment. Now apply sharing, caring and conserving to your housing. Halve square-footage by renting bedrooms or downsizing; extend useful life by painting, repairing leaks and solving moisture problems; and reduce energy by sealing drafts and boosting insulation.

Taking this concept of multiplication a step further, consider its application to an institutional building. If we were to assume that over 20 years, a plan would:

A Reduce the area per occupant by 20%

T Upgrade the technology of systems to enhance efficiency by 30%

E Upgrade the building's insulation and reduce drafts by 30%

O Improve operational sensors and timers to heat/cool/ventilate only when needed by 30%

M   Manage building schedule to have less empty space by 20%

U   Inspire sustainable user habits to reduce impact by 20%

L   Care for building and extend useful life by 30%

F   Use cleaner fuels with lower emissions/BTU by 20%

C   Use solar, wind, geothermal, landfill gas and hydroelectric by 30%

In this example, each factor is relatively independent, resulting in multiplying benefits. In 20 years, this building's emissions could be calculated as follows:

$$\begin{array}{l} A\,(0.8) \times T\,(0.7) \times \\ E\,(0.7) \times O\,(0.7) \times \\ M\,(0.8) \times U\,(0.8) \times \\ L\,(0.7) \times F\,(0.8) \times C\,(0.7) \end{array} = \begin{array}{l} \text{0.069 or roughly 7\% of} \\ \text{the original emissions,} \\ \text{a 93\% reduction.} \end{array}$$

At this point, installing more wind, solar and hydroelectric energy are feasible ways to bring this building close to carbon neutral. Notice that we haven't purchased carbon credits yet or made dirty deals like trading toxic waste for reduced carbon (nuclear) or taken land from food production and habitat to decrease dependency on foreign oil (biofuels).

While some argue that the technology is not yet ready, others, including the College of the Atlantic, announced carbon neutrality on December 19, 2007, through the purchase of offsets, low-impact hydroelectric power and on-campus energy reductions. The University of New Hampshire's COGEN plant reduced emissions by 21 percent, and when its 12.7-mile pipeline to the landfill is complete in 2009, combined GHG reductions are estimated at 67 percent.

Technical feasibility is not the issue. Willingness is. What might motivate political, institutional and business leaders to take on such reduction programs? Decision-makers' receptiveness to sustainability modulates with energy bills. When oil was $30 per barrel in 2000, sustainability was barely part of the daily lexicon. When the price soared to over $100 per barrel in 2008, reaching a high of $145 on July 3, 2008, bike tires got pumped.

It's unlikely that prices will return to $30 per barrel. There's a better chance that politicians and big business will push for nuclear power, coal, biofuels, wars and offshore drilling. If they're successful, increased consumerism would further accelerate species extinction and climate change. For them to fail, the public must shift its priorities.

My open agenda with college students is to exploit the fact that they are caring, thoughtful individuals ready to be part of the solution. Change happens when the pain associated with contributing to the demise of our children's future becomes unbearable, when our own emptiness becomes toxic to our spirit. Change happens when our love for the world, for nature, for ourselves is owned.

Radical sustainability doesn't have to save us money to motivate us. It is simply the right thing to do. It is honest, fun and wholesome. Even with intense motivation, knowledge of alternatives and a supportive community, we can't escape society's glitter, even as it destroys the planet. Its lure is powerful and omnipresent.

The pulse I get on my fellow Americans is that the status quo is like an 80-pound pack wearing them out. You'd be hard-pressed to find a few people who think that their children's future is healthy, safe or sustainable. Many people are stressed and overwhelmed. They're fearful of what's to come, even if unconsciously so. Channeled positively, that fear leads to a desire to make the world sustainable, to take collective action similar to the planting of victory gardens in World War II.

The stakes now are even higher, as we hope for a mass movement to save the masses. Meanwhile, our days slip by, often occupied with unsustainable activities and work that isn't vital. This dissonance creates anxiety, resignation, cynicism and, at its worst, depression. Working with students, I've noticed how creative and dedicated they become when solving tough, real-life problems. A coherent mass movement is really here, but it's not televised.

Simplicity. Sustainability. Less really is more. Hoist that 30-pound pack and cinch the waist belt. It's going to be a fun and fulfilling trip.

Downshifting to a Carbon-friendly Economy

by Juliet Schor

JULIET SCHOR, now a professor of sociology at Boston College, taught at Harvard University for 17 years in the Department of Economics and the Committee on Degrees in Women's Studies. She wrote *Born to Buy: The Commercialized Child and the New Consumer Culture*, *The Overworked American: The Unexpected Decline of Leisure* and *The Overspent American: Why We Want What We Don't Need*.

L ET ME START with a controversial idea — that per capita consumption needs to decline in the US to achieve sustainable levels of greenhouse gas emissions (GHG).

To help think about why, consider the problem from the perspective of the IPAT accounting framework that decomposes ecological impact into three factors — population (P), per capita consumption (represented by A, or affluence) and ecological impact per unit of consumption (or represented by T, or technology). To date, the debate, and particularly the policy debate, has focused on mechanisms for reducing T, primarily through a shift toward cleaner, renewable sources of energy. Such a shift, along with various forms of conservation (building insulation, higher gas mileage, etc.) is essential. But there are reasons to believe that technological change is a necessary but not sufficient aspect of a solution. First, the magnitude of necessary GHG reduction is so large that multiple approaches will be necessary. Second, the business-as-usual path for consumption is to continue on its average path of roughly three percent increase per year. This means that technologically induced reductions need to take place on an exponential path. Finally, a related point is that when technological improvements in energy efficiency do occur, they are often counterbalanced or overridden by increases in scale. In the US since 1970, this scenario appears to have occurred in vehicles, where better per-vehicle mileage has been wiped out by more miles driven per capita, and in residential energy use, where efficiency improvements have been overridden by an increase in appliances and overall demand. Predictions from proponents of approaches, such as Factor Four, eco-efficiency and zero waste, have proved to be overly optimistic. Achieving requisite reductions in GHGs will require an alteration in the path of consumption.

This claim is a "third rail" in American politics, and I do not suggest it lightly. However, there are approaches that would allow us to gradually transition to an economy that meets people's needs, works well from an economic point of view and is characterized by stable or falling per capita consumption, at least until carbon-neutral growth is a reality. I believe that, in the last year or two, the political space to talk about these solutions has expanded, and it will continue to do so as the nation squarely faces the realities of climate change.

Downshifting and the Movement to Trade Money for Time

The key to downshifting the consumption trajectory is through the path of income. This is largely because the propensity to spend out of current income is very high, for all but the wealthy. The savings rate in the US is now one percent or less. Efforts to increase savings, while laudable for a variety of reasons, will have only limited impacts. Structural mechanisms, such as changing the default options on workplace and other savings plans, are far more effective, because they divert income before it finds its way into the consumer's pocket. However, even if there is a substantial increase in the savings rate, the net effect on GHGs may not be as intended. Higher household savings are likely to end up as demand somewhere else in the economic system, and will not necessarily yield a reduced overall level of economic activity and emissions.

A more effective intervention will be to cut the link between productivity growth and income growth. Over time, economies expand either through extensive growth (pulling in more people, more land or other resources) or intensive growth (using existing resources more productively). In advanced economies, productivity growth is key to success and the functioning of the economy. It will be the foundation of a sustainable economy, particularly as new mechanisms for creating productivity growth in the use of natural capital are developed.

When productivity growth occurs, for example, in labor inputs, it can be used to either produce more output from a given number of labor hours, or labor hours can be reduced while still generating the original level of productivity. For the last 50 years, productivity growth has largely been used to expand output. Indeed, the principle of using productivity growth to raise incomes was built into some labor contracts (wages grew by the rate of productivity). Since 1960, per capita gross national product has increased even more than productivity. Elsewhere I have termed this a "cycle of work and spend," because higher productivity leads to more income and spending and then consumer preferences adapt or habituate to that higher spending level.

The key to achieving a more sustainable path for consumption is to translate productivity growth into shorter hours of work instead of more income. This gives employees a tangible benefit that significant numbers say they would prefer to more income. It provides a vital undersupplied resource to communities and families (non-marketed labor time), and it avoids the additional ecological and climate footprint associated with more consumption.

Another key aspect of this solution should be noted. As research in behavioral economics has shown, individuals are highly averse to income losses. For that reason, proposals to "reduce consumption" or "reduce income" will be politically unpopular. However, individuals value future income far less than they value current income. Therefore, the key to a politically viable strategy for controlling per capita consumption is to cut off the "spigot" of increases in income and offer increases in something else instead. Foregoing hypothetical raises is a lot easier psychologically, particularly if the quid pro quo is a four-day workweek or other reduced work-time options.

A few key policy changes are necessary to facilitate this path. I have discussed these elsewhere, so I will just mention them briefly. First is to shift per-person costs of employment either to a per-hour basis or to finance them outside the firm. Healthcare costs are the most important of these per-person non-wage compensation costs. Second, a shift from payment by yearly or monthly salary to an hourly wage will also facilitate the growth of time for income activity. And finally, improvements in the distribution of income will reduce the pressure for longer hours that is coming from those parts of the income distribution that are losing out. Controlling these incentives for both firms and individuals will allow a genuine "market in hours" to develop. That then will be the basis of more widespread voluntary downshifting.

Economic Performance in a Downshifting Economy

There is a widespread perception that market economies need to grow in order to be successful. I have always found this claim curious, because it is not a view that comes from standard economic theory. Some aspects of economic performance need to be addressed in slow-growing or steady-state economies, most notably productivity growth. But in general, a healthy well-functioning economy is compatible with a path of aggregate output that is not growing. It is important to remember that I am discussing the aggregate level of output, not the revenues or size of individual firms, which will of course grow. But aggregate output, an abstract concept in any case, does not need to expand annually.

In the case of what I am calling a "downshifting" economy, the key to its viability is dynamics in the labor market. If people begin to trade income for time, and withdraw hours from the labor market, then the amount of consumer demand necessary to provide for full employment is reduced commensurately. (The key here is that the consumer demand and labor market sides move together.) Downshifters earn less money, they demand fewer products, and they need fewer hours of work to reproduce their standards of living. The economy gradually transitions to a lower per capita level of hours worked, consumption and ecological impact. This path does not yield recession, lower wages or fewer jobs. Indeed, depending on how the policy aspects of the transition are managed, it can expand employment opportunities by reducing the average number of hours worked in every job (in contrast to the rise in hours per full-time job that has occurred in recent decades).

There are a few keys to making this transition successfully. One is that the changes are gradual. The second is that they are based on enhanced choices in the labor market to trade income for time. That will require alternative health-care financing, changes in compensation policies and provision for career paths that do not require full-time hours. There also needs to be ample public support for technological research and development and education spending. These are the keys to maintaining high rates of productivity growth in a macro environment of slow or no aggregate growth.

Can "Downshifting" Be a Politically Viable Path?

If implemented properly, policies to encourage trading time for money can be both popular and climate enhancing. Average annual working hours have risen substantially in recent decades, particularly once structural under- and unemployment have been controlled for. A significant number of Americans are experiencing time shortages and would welcome labor market policies that facilitate their trading income for time, particularly if they are not forced to take significant career penalties. For example, polling by the Center for a New American Dream has found between one-third (36%) and one-half (52%) of a national sample responded affirmatively to various proposals to trade income for time. Proposals for an additional day off per week are particularly popular. Now a growing body of survey data supports the idea that a significant number of Americans would respond affirmatively to opportunities to work less.

The key to getting onto a lower consumption trajectory is to focus on tradeoffs for future income, putting structural mechanisms in place to channel productivity growth into shorter hours, and to put the other policy supports in place (health insurance) that make these lifestyle decisions viable for individuals and households. Such a path is very family friendly, and can be incorporated as part of a response to climate change that enhances families, communities and quality of life at the same time that it reduces GHG emissions.

What's the
Economy for, Anyway?

by John de Graaf

JOHN DE GRAAF is the national coordinator of the Take
Back Your Time campaign, co-author of *Affluenza: The
All-Consuming Epidemic* and editor of *Take Back Your
Time: Fighting Overwork and Time Poverty in America*.
He is also a filmmaker and recently co-produced *The
Motherhood Manifesto*.

John regrets that, to the eternal disappointment of
his mother, he left college just before graduation to become a community organizer. In penance, he vowed to
live simply, a decision reinforced by his profession as a
documentary filmmaker.

If they can get you asking the wrong question,
they don't have to worry about the answers.

— THOMAS PYNCHON, *GRAVITY'S RAINBOW*

SUGGEST ANY alternative to the status quo these days —
greater environmental protection, for example, or
shorter working hours — and the first question reporters
are likely to ask is, "But what will that do to the economy?"
Immediately, advocates must try to prove that their sugges-
tions will not adversely affect economic growth or the Dow
Jones industrial average.

It's long past time for a new framing offensive, one that turns the obligatory question on its head and shifts the burden of proof to those who resist change. Imagine bumper stickers, posters, Internet messages, a thousand inquiries visible everywhere, asking a different question.

What's the Economy for, Anyway?

It's time to demand that champions of the status quo defend their implicit answer to that question. Do they actually believe that the purpose of the economy is to achieve the grossest domestic product and allow the richest among us to multiply their treasures without limits? For in practice, that really is their answer.

But what if we answer the question differently, perhaps as Gifford Pinchot, the first chief of the US Forest Service, did a century ago? His answer was, "The greatest good for the greatest number over the long run."

In that light, economic success cannot be measured by gross domestic product (GDP) or stock prices alone. It must take into account the other values that constitute the greatest good — health, happiness, knowledge, kindness — for the greatest number — equality, access to opportunity — over the long run, in a healthy democracy and sustainable environment.

Historical Background

It's time to set America back on course.

After increasing social equality and greatly improving health and other quality-of-life measures (including major increases in leisure time) from World War II until the mid-1970s, the United States abruptly changed its economic trajectory.

"It will be a hard pill for many Americans to swallow," *Business Week* predicted in October 1974, "the idea of doing with less so that big business can have more. Nothing that this nation or any other nation has done in modern history compares in difficulty with the selling job that must now be done to make people accept the new reality."

Emboldened by Richard Nixon's landslide 1972 victory, extreme conservatives moved to reduce the responsibilities (and increase the wealth) of wealthy Americans, while cutting back on public services for the poor and average working Americans. These policies accelerated during the 1980s and early 1990s and are now enshrined in the "you're on your ownership" attitude of the present federal policies.

Meanwhile, Western European nations took a different course, maintaining their social contracts and at least modestly improving their safety nets for the poor. Their provision of more public goods — health care, education, transportation, common space, etc. — supported by higher and more progressive taxation measures than in the United States reduced the need (or desire) of individuals to maximize their own incomes.

So What Happened?

First, in terms of productivity per worker hour, Western Europeans nearly closed the gap with the United States. They were producing, on average, 65 percent as much as Americans produced per hour in 1970. By 2000, their productivity was 95 percent that of Americans. But on the other hand, their consumption of goods and services, measured in GDP per capita, remained where it was in 1970 — roughly 70 percent that of Americans.

There is a simple explanation for this seeming anomaly: European working hours, which in 1970 were slightly longer than those of Americans, dropped to about 80 percent of US hours. We could say that Europeans traded major portions of their productivity increases for free time instead of money, while Americans — consciously or otherwise — put all their gains into increasing their per capita GDP.

Pose the question, "What did that do to the economy?" and the answer appears clear — Americans, with a much bigger GDP, are the obvious winners.

But ask instead, "What is the economy for anyway?" and a different answer emerges. For most of the final quarter of the 20th century, Europeans improved their quality of life relative to Americans in almost every measure.

Health

While American health has improved in absolute terms since the 1970s, the United States once ranked near the top in terms of overall health. It now rates below that of every other industrial country, despite spending by far the highest percentage of GDP on health care.

Equality

If one looks at equality, a similar pattern emerges. The US, which was near the median among industrial countries in terms of economic equality in 1974, now has the widest gap between rich and poor.

Savings

Savings are a key indicator of security for many people. While American personal savings rates (10%) were slightly higher than those of Europeans in 1970, they have dropped to negative numbers (−1.6% last year), while European Union (EU) citizens now save an average of 12 percent of their incomes.

Sustainability

European progress has also come at a lower cost to the environment. While EU nations were choosing more leisure time rather than working harder to close the consumer gap with Americans, they also took greater steps toward sustainability.

The result is that EU countries require only half the energy consumption per capita as that of Americans, while producing 70 percent as many goods and services. The average American has an ecological footprint (the productive land and water necessary to produce his or her lifestyle) of 24 acres; for Europeans, the average is 12 acres.

One can find similar results in many other areas of quality of life, including: levels of trust, crime, incarceration, family breakdown, literacy, happiness indicators, preschool education and even access to information technologies.

Tellingly, the Genuine Progress Indicator — an alternative to the GDP developed by Redefining Progress that measures 24 quality-of-life indices — shows a fairly consistent decline in well-being in the United States since a peak in 1973. Similar indices for Europe show consistent improvement in most areas of life, even if increases are sometimes slow or spotty.

Meeting Our Needs

One model for judging the success of the economy is to see how well it allows citizens to meet their needs as outlined by psychologist Abraham Maslow. In his often-cited hierarchy of needs theory, Maslow suggested that humans must first adequately satisfy such basic needs as food, shelter, health and safety and "belongingness" before moving on to what he called "higher" or "meta" needs.

In the early 1970s, Maslow suggested that, as a society, the United States had met nearly all its citizens' physiological and safety needs and was moving to satisfy higher needs as well. Ironically, by such a standard, we have lost ground rather than gained it — we have more citizens living in poverty and a much greater overall sense of insecurity today than we did then, despite more than a 60 percent increase in real per capita GDP.

Most Americans know intrinsically that increases in GDP do not mean economic success if health outcomes and social connections continue to decline relative to other countries.

This is why we must raise the question, What is the economy for, anyway? to a crescendo that cannot be ignored by the media or our political leaders. Only when we begin to ask the right question can we hope to find answers that can improve our quality of life.

We must then ask, What roles do the market, the state, non-governmental organizations and our common wealth respectively have to play in achieving the greatest good for the greatest number over the long run?

Inevitably, even sympathetic reporters and others will ask us, Can we change the economy in the ways the Europeans have and still compete in the global economy? The answer, quite simply, is yes.

According to the World Economic Forum, the United States ranks second in world economic competitiveness. So it's possible to do things our way — reducing government, slashing taxes, cutting the safety net and widening the divide between rich and poor — and be competitive.

But is it necessary? Consider that the other four most competitive nations are Finland (ranked first), Sweden, Denmark and Norway. In fact, European nations make up most of the top ten. All are far more globalized and far more subject to international competitive pressures than we are and have been for many years. And all of them are far more egalitarian than the United States.

Finland has, in fact, the smallest gap between rich and poor of any nation. The Finnish social safety net is a generous one, and workers enjoy a great deal of leisure time — an average of 30 days of paid vacation. The story is similar in other European countries. Clearly, it is possible to have a more just and people-friendly economy and compete globally.

Imagine seeing our simple question, What's the economy for, anyway? everywhere — in print, posters, on bumper stickers, on websites — or hearing it asked over and over on TV, radio and in forums and debates. It might be seen as a Trojan horse, seemingly innocent, but remarkably subversive.

The point of all this is not simply to change this or that specific policy, but to create a different thought context by which we might begin to change the entire trend toward privatization and inequality. The point is to show that current "common sense" about economics is "non-sense" if our goal is a better quality of life that is sustainable over the long run.

When we forget to ask, What is the economy for, anyway? we leave ourselves open to the GDP worship of so many of our leaders. When we ask the question over and over and demand answers, we open possibilities for a new and better world.

[Note: First published in *The New American Dream*, newdream.org/newsletter/economy_for.php.]

We Are Hard-wired
to Care and Connect

by David Korten

DAVID KORTEN is co-founder and board chair of the Positive Futures Network, which publishes *YES!* magazine, president of the People-Centered Development Forum and a board member of the Business Alliance for Local Living Economies (BALLE). His books include *The Great Turning: From Empire to Earth Community*, the international best-seller *When Corporations Rule the World* and *The Post-Corporate World: Life after Capitalism*. David has an MBA and PhD from the Stanford University Graduate School of Business, served as a Harvard Business School professor and, for 30 years, worked as a development professional in Asia, Africa and Latin America. His early thinking on the need to simplify was influenced in part by E. F. Schumacher's *Small Is Beautiful*.

FOR ALL THE cultural differences reflected in our richly varied customs, languages, religions and political ideologies, psychologically healthy humans share a number of core values and aspirations. Although we may differ in our idea of the "how," we want healthy, happy children, loving families and a caring community with a beautiful, healthy natural environment. We want a world of cooperation, justice and peace and a say in the decisions that affect our lives. The shared values of Purple America manifest this shared human dream. It is the true American dream undistorted by corporate media, advertisers and political demagogues — the dream we must now actualize if there is to be a human future.

For the past 5,000 years, we humans have devoted much creative energy to perfecting our capacity for greed and violence — a practice that has been enormously costly for our children, families, communities and nature. Now, on the verge of environmental and social collapse, we face an imperative to bring the world of our dreams into being by cultivating our long-suppressed, even denied, capacity for sharing and compassion.

Despite the constant mantra that "There is no alternative" to greed and competition, daily experience and a growing body of scientific evidence support the thesis that we humans are born to connect, learn and serve and that it is indeed within our means to:

- create family-friendly communities in which we get our satisfaction from caring relationships rather than material consumption,
- achieve the ideal, which traces back to Aristotle, of creating democratic middle-class societies without extremes of wealth and poverty and
- form a global community of nations committed to restoring the health of the planet and sharing Earth's bounty to the long-term benefit of all.

The first step toward achieving the world we want is to acknowledge that there is an alternative to our current human course. We humans are not hopelessly divided and doomed to self-destruct by a genetic predisposition toward greed and violence. Culture, the system of customary beliefs, value and perceptions that encodes our shared learning, gives humans an extraordinary capacity to choose our destiny. It does not assure that we will use this capacity wisely, but it does give us the means to change course by conscious collective choice.

The Story in Our Head

The primary barrier to achieving our common dream is in fact a story that endlessly loops in our heads telling us that a world of peace and sharing is contrary to our nature — a naïve fantasy forever beyond reach. There are many variations, but this is the essence:

> It is our human nature to be competitive, individualistic, and materialistic. Our well-being depends on strong leaders with the will to use police and military powers to protect us from one another, and on the competitive forces of a free, unregulated market to channel our individual greed to constructive ends. The competition for survival and dominance — violent and destructive as it may be — is the driving force of evolution. It has been the key to human success since the beginning of time, assures that the most worthy rise to leadership and ultimately works to the benefit of everyone.

I call this our Empire story because it affirms the system of dominator hierarchy that has held sway for 5,000 years (see *YES!*, Summer 2006, *5,000 Years of Empire*). Underlying the economic and scientific versions of this story is a religious story that promises that enduring violence and injustice in this life will be rewarded with eternal peace, harmony and bliss in the afterlife.

To reinforce the Empire myth, corporate media bombard us with reports of greed and violence, and celebrate as cultural heroes materially successful, but morally challenged, politicians and corporate CEOs who exhibit a callous disregard for the human and environmental consequences of their actions.

Never mind the story's moral contradictions and its conflict with our own experience with caring and trustworthy friends, family and strangers. It serves to keep us confused, uncertain and dependent on establishment-sanctioned moral authorities to tell us what is right and true. It also supports policies and institutions that actively undermine development of the caring, sharing relationships essential to responsible citizenship in a functioning democratic society. Fortunately, there is a more positive story that can put us on the road to recovery. It is supported by recent scientific findings, our daily experience and the ageless teachings of the great religious prophets.

Wired to Connect

Scientists who use advanced imaging technology to study brain function report that the human brain is wired to reward caring, cooperation and service. According to this research, merely thinking about another person experiencing harm triggers the same reaction in our brain as when a mother sees distress in her baby's face. Conversely, the act of helping another triggers the brain's pleasure center and benefits our health by boosting our immune system, reducing our heart rate and preparing us to approach and soothe. Positive emotions like compassion produce similar benefits. By contrast, negative emotions suppress our immune system, increase heart rate and prepare us to fight or flee.

These findings are consistent with the pleasure most of us experience from being a member of an effective team or extending an uncompensated helping hand to another human. It is entirely logical. If our brains were not wired for life in community, our species would have expired long ago. We have an instinctual desire to protect the group, including its weakest and most vulnerable members — its children. Behavior contrary to this positive norm is an indicator of serious social and psychological dysfunction.

Happiness Is a Caring Community

These neurological findings are corroborated by social science findings that, beyond the minimum level of income essential to meet basic needs, membership in a cooperative, caring community is a far better predictor of happiness and emotional health than the size of one's paycheck or bank account. Perhaps the most impressive evidence comes from studies conducted by University of Illinois professor Ed Diener, and others, comparing the life-satisfaction scores of groups of people of radically different financial means. Four groups with almost identical scores on a seven-point scale were clustered at the top.

Consistent with the Empire story that material consumption is the key to happiness, those on *Forbes* magazine's list of richest Americans had an average score of 5.8. They were in a statistical tie, however, with three groups known for their modest lifestyles and strength of community: the Pennsylvania Amish (5.8) who favor horses over cars and tractors; the Inuit of Northern Greenland (5.9), an indigenous hunting and fishing people; and the Masai (5.7), a traditional herding people in East Africa who live without electricity or running water in huts fashioned from dried cow dung. Apparently, it takes a very great deal of money to produce the happiness that comes with being a member of a caring community with a strong sense of place. The evidence suggests we could all be a lot healthier and happier if we put less emphasis on making money and more on cultivating caring community.

The Purple American desire to create a society of healthy children, families, communities and natural systems is no fluke. It is an expression of our deepest and most positive human impulses, a sign that we may overall be a healthier and less divisive society than our dysfunctional politics suggest.

Learning to Be Human

If the properly functioning human brain is wired for caring, cooperation and service, how do we account for the outrageous greed and violence that threaten our collective survival? Here we encounter our distinctive human capacity to suppress or facilitate the development of the higher-order function of the human brain essential to responsible adult citizenship.

We humans have a complex three-part brain. The base is the "reptilian" brain that coordinates basic functions, such as breathing, hunting and eating, reproducing, protecting territory and engaging the fight-or-flight response. These functions are essential to survival and an authentic part of our humanity, but they express the most primitive and least-evolved part of our brain, which advertisers and political demagogues have learned to manipulate by playing to our basest fears and desires.

Layered on top of the reptilian brain is the limbic or "mammalian" brain, the center of the emotional intelligence that gives mammals their distinctive capacity to experience emotion, read the emotional state of other mammals, bond socially, care for their children and form cooperative communities.

The third and largest layer is the neocortical brain, the center of our capacity for cognitive reasoning, symbolic thought, awareness and self-aware volition. This layer distinguishes our species from other mammals. Its full, beneficial function depends, however, on the complementary functions of our reptilian and mammalian brains.

Most of the development of the limbic and neocortical brains essential to actualizing the capacities that make us most distinctively human occurs after birth and depends on lifelong learning acquired through our interactions with family, community and nature. Developmental psychologists describe the healthy pathway to a fully formed human consciousness as a progression from the self-centered, undifferentiated magical consciousness of the newborn to the fully mature, inclusive and multidimensional spiritual consciousness of the wise elder.

Realizing the fullness of our humanity depends on the balanced development of the empathetic limbic and cognitive neocortical brains to establish their primacy over the primitive unsocialized instincts of the reptilian brain. Tragically, most modern societies neglect or even suppress this development.

A depersonalized economic system with no attachment to place disrupts the bonds of community and family and makes it nearly impossible for parents to provide their children with the nurturing attention essential to the healthy development of their limbic brains. Educational systems that focus on rote learning organized by fragmented disciplines fail to develop our potential for critical holistic thinking. Leaving social learning to peer groups lacking the benefit of adult mentors limits development of a mature, morally grounded social intelligence. We are conducting an unintended evolutionary experiment in producing a line of highly intelligent but emotionally challenged reptiles wielding technologies capable of disrupting or even terminating the entire evolutionary enterprise.

The Power of Conversation

Getting out of our current mess begins with a conversation to change the shared cultural story about our essential nature. The women's movement offers an instructive lesson.

In little more than a decade, a few courageous women changed the cultural story that the key to a woman's happiness is to find the right man, marry him and devote her life to his service. As Cecile Andrews, author of *Circle of Simplicity*, relates, the transition to a new gender story began with discussion circles in which women came together in their living rooms to share their stories. Until then, a woman whose experience failed to conform to the prevailing story assumed that the problem was a deficiency in herself. As women shared their own stories, each realized that the flaw was in the story. Millions of women were soon spreading a new gender story that has unleashed the feminine as a powerful force for global transformation.

The Voluntary Simplicity movement organizes similar opportunities for people to share their stories about what makes them truly happy. The fallacy of the story that material consumption is the path to happiness is quickly exposed and replaced with the fact that we truly come alive as we reduce material consumption and gain control of our time to nurture the relationships that bring true happiness.

We must now begin a similar process to affirm that those of us who choose to cooperate rather than compete are not fighting human nature. We are, instead, developing the part of our humanity that gives us the best chance, not merely for survival, but for happiness.

The process of changing the powerful stories that limit our lives begins with conversation in our living room, library, church, mosque or synagogue. By speaking and listening to each other, we begin to discover the true potentials of our human nature and our common vision of the world. It is not a new conversation. Isolated groups of humans have engaged in it for millennia. What is new is the fact that the communications technologies now in place create the possibility of ending the isolation and melding our local conversations into a global one that can break the self-replicating spiral of competitive violence of 5,000 years of Empire.

As this conversation brings a critical mass of people to the realization that the Empire story is both false and devastatingly destructive, we can turn as a species from perfecting our capacity for exclusionary competition to perfecting our capacity for inclusionary cooperation. We can create a cultural story that says competition and polarization, whether the red-blue political divide or the rich-poor economic one, is not the inevitable result of being human. It is the result of suppressing the healthiest part of our humanity.

There are no trade-offs here. The institutional and cultural transformation required to avert environmental and social collapse is the same as the transformation required to nurture the development of the empathetic limbic brain, unleash the creative potentials of the human consciousness and create the world we want. It is an extraordinary convergence between our reptilian interest in survival, our mammalian interest in bonding and our human interest in cultivating the potentials of our self-reflective consciousness.

[Note: David Korten wrote this article as part of *Purple America*, the Fall 2008 issue of *YES! Magazine*.]

AFTERWORD

Time to Talk!

Creating Simplicity Conversation Circles

by Cecile Andrews

A nation can be maintained only if, between the state and the individual, there is interposed a whole series of secondary groups near enough to the individuals to attract them strongly in their sphere of action and drag them, in this way, into the general torment of civil life.

— EMILE DURKHEIM

L ATELY I'VE HEARD pundits asking if the "new" desire to save money in reaction to a shaky economy could be a real change or just a blip in history. Most conclude that it's only a blip because it's human nature to always want more. In the long run nothing will change.

However, as we've seen, it's also human nature to care for others and to join others in community. We're wired to connect. People's behavior is part "nature" and part environment. In other words, we're capable of being many different things depending on the forces that affect us. As we've seen, our economy encourages us to be cutthroat and competitive. Naturally people compete for wealth.

But we're at a unique place in history now. We really don't have a choice. Climate change demands a change. But there could be different kinds of changes. One scenerio involves an expansion of what we have — cutthroat competition and wars for dwindling resources, the "every man for himself" philosophy. The other is a commitment to the common good, the idea that we're all in this together. One accepts a greater wealth gap; the other pursues an egalitarian society. We have evidence that the first scenerio has failed. We must work for the second.

To do that, we must transform people's belief systems. Unless people have a different view of "the good life," we'll continue with our destructive pursuit of more. We must come to believe that less is more.

As we look for ways to change our value system, it's inspiring to read some of Franklin Roosevelt's words. In his first Thanksgiving Proclamation in 1933, he said, "May we ask guidance in more surely learning the ancient truth that greed and selfishness and striving for undue riches can never bring lasting happiness or good to the individual or to his neighbors."

In his 1935 Thanksgiving proclamation, he said, "In traversing a period of national stress our country has been knit together in a closer fellowship of mutual interest and common purpose. We can well be grateful that more and more of our people understand and seek the greater good of the greater number. We can be grateful that selfish purpose of personal gain, at our neighbor's loss, less strongly asserts itself."

How do we move our culture to Roosevelt's belief system? It's difficult. For instance, many of us are aware of the happiness research. We "know" that being rich won't make us happy. We've read the literature that shows that lottery winners are ecstatic the first week, but by the end of the year, they are no happier than before and, in fact, may be less happy. But even with this knowledge, most of us think that if we won the lottery, we'd be an exception! Our belief that wealth equals happiness is very, very deep.

So as we think about change, we must move beyond trying to change people with facts! Just telling people that we're destroying the planet doesn't seem to bring about change! Just telling people being rich won't make them happy doesn't work. How do we get Americans to turn away from their materialism?

First, we need to understand why we're materialists. There are a multitude of reasons, but in particular, we were formed by America's early years of lonesome cowboys and isolated farmers — the original rugged individualists. We came to believe the idea that "You're on your own. Every man for himself." People who do not look to others for their security naturally turn to material things.

Further, we are not a reflective people. We've always loved taking action, not sitting around and talking. We're restless and impatient with the slow pace of thinking. So, throughout the years, we've failed to examine our choices and bolted after every new thing.

Thus, we are driven to consume by our lack of connectedness and our lack of reflection. To change, we must find a way to counter these tendencies: We must give people an experience of community and deliberation. We need to come together for joyful, caring dialogue! It's time to talk!

Each creative society has had conversation at its core. The Greeks gathered in the Athenaeum to discuss freedom and democracy, the 18th-century English thinkers met in coffee houses, and the French Revolution was born in the salons.

In early America, Benjamin Franklin organized a club called the Junto, which met each week for discussion and planning. In the 1850s, Emerson, Lowell, Hawthorne, Whittier, Longfellow and Oliver Wendall Holmes formed the Saturday Club, meeting on the last Saturday afternoon of each month to eat and talk together. William James and Oliver Wendall Holmes referred in their writings to their Metaphysical Club. Margaret Fuller led Conversations for women, including people such as early women's rights leader Elizabeth Cady Stanton.

In these groups, people experienced community and reflection. Of course, we're talking about democracy, our American lifeblood. Community and reflection are the core of democracy. On his 90th birthday, American philosopher John Dewey said, "Democracy is born in conversation." Today's great movements of democracy grew because people talked to each other. How do you think people learned of the Montgomery bus boycott that was inspired by Rosa Parks and catapulted Martin Luther King into his leadership role? People passed the word around themselves and joined together in a powerful community effort. The 20th-century women's movement was fueled by consciousness-raising groups, where women gathered in church basements and tiny cramped apartments and talked with each other and told the truth about their lives and felt connected in the way they never had before.

Conversation and reflection fueled all of the revolutions in our country, and it can fuel our Simplicity movement. In particular, we can learn from the Civil Rights movement. Not long before her historic action, Rosa Parks attended a community school called Highlander. The work of Highlander lies behind much of the civil rights movement and involved people such as Martin Luther King and Eleanor Roosevelt. But mostly it involved the common people talking with each other. Highlander's philosophy: The wisdom is in the people. You bring people together and have them talk about their problems, and they will find the answers. People talked together, then went out and took action as a community. This is what democracy is.

And so, it is in this tradition that I've worked to create and form Simplicity Conversation Circles. (Since the publication of my book *Circle of Simplicity*, hundreds of Simplicity Circles have formed. With the renewed interest in Simplicity, once again they're on the rise.)

Essentially, these gatherings are the essence of the heart of Simplicity. You cannot live simply unless you are engaged in deliberation. Without deliberation you will be manipulated by the advertisers, the politicians, the schools and the churches. Simplicity is making conscious choices — something that demands deliberation.

And today, Nobel Prize winner Al Gore sees deliberation as essential in our crisis of climate change. In his book *Assault on Reason*, he talks about "A Well-connected Citizenry":

> And in today's world, that means recognizing that it's impossible to have a well-informed citizenry without having a well-connected citizenry. While education remains important, it is now connection that is the key. A well-connected citizenry is made up of men and women who discuss and debate ideas and issues among themselves and who constantly test the validity of the information and impressions they receive from one another — as well as the ones they receive from their government. No citizenry can be well informed without a constant flow of honest information about contemporary events and without a full opportunity to participate in a discussion of

the choices that the society must make…a priority should be placed on reconnecting the American people to the substance of the deliberative process.

Engaging in conversation and community, talking about the ideas in this book can be a part of that deliberative process that Gore speaks of. And so, as we work to create a culture of Simplicity, we are also working to help democracy endure. Simplicity and democracy live or die together.

Community Education

In my work as an educator, I've discovered certain basic truths. First, *facts are not enough*. We need to set people's spirits on fire. We must enliven as well as enlighten. We must inspire and motivate people to care about the common good. We inspire people by bringing them together to experience the acceptance and belongingness of community. People become inspired when they have real conversations with others.

Second, *we want people to learn to trust their own judgment and speak out*, to refuse to be silenced and intimidated by those who claim to be authorities and experts. People learn this by contemplating their own experience, telling their own stories and learning from each other. We must come to believe that wisdom lies in people, and this knowledge only comes when we experience conversation and community.

Third, *we want to help people think critically*, to spot the sham, manipulation and false promises that undermine the greater good. Usually people keep silent about the things they see. They don't want to be labeled a crackpot, and they're not sure they're right. But in a safe environment, they reveal their perceptions and have them validated. Too often, we're like the people who admired the Emperor's new

clothes — no one spoke up about what they were truly seeing. But when people have a chance to share their views,
they discover they're not alone and they're not crazy!

Finally, *people need to experience connectedness and belonging*. This happens when there is conversation between
equals — informal, convivial, congenial conversation. These
are conversations, not discussions, because in discussions
we usually try to "win," arguing and attacking each other. In
conversations we listen to each other, learn from each other
and enjoy each other.

Using *Less is More* for Simplicity Circles

Less Is More is the perfect book for Simplicity Conversation Circles! The essays are short, relevant and quick reading. Just get together a few friends or form a group at work,
school or church. You don't need trained leaders because
the approach is informal and conversational. There is a
merely a coordinator, a person who convenes the group
and keeps things on track. Some circles meet every week or
every other week. Meeting only once a month makes it difficult to build community.

There are a few important things to remember, though.
When beginning a group, draw up some reminders of good
conversation; for instance, no arguments. The purpose is
convivial conversation, not winning a boxing match. Ask
people to keep it short! In our Simplicity Circles, we often
pass around three-minute egg timers.

Ask people to read one essay for each meeting and come
prepared to discuss *one* idea that grabbed them, something
that connected to their own experience. It's vital that they
have the opportunity to talk in groups of three or four; in
a larger group, only a few will talk. Encourage people to go
around the circle, talking about the idea that's important
to them and considering its ramifications. Discuss what

changes are needed — including personal change, community change and policy change. Finally, members should decide what individual actions they will take and set a goal for the week. It should be a very, very small action — something they are able to follow through on! At the end of the small group discussions, everyone comes together to talk about the actions that they are planning to take. At the beginning of the next meeting, members will report on their actions.

Thus, in a Simplicity Conversation Circle, we work for personal and political change, we begin to learn to trust our own judgment, we learn to think critically about the broader society, and we learn to take action. Ultimately people begin to believe in themselves and to feel inspired to continue to work for broader democratic change.

So use this book! Don't just read it! Start a Simplicity Conversation Circle! Create a culture of deliberation, with conversation and community! People discover that coming together to talk about ideas and social change is one of the most exciting, enjoyable things they can do! Who wants to wander the sterile shopping malls or watch soulless television when they can make a difference and enjoy themselves through the age old delight of conversation!

Ultimately, community deliberation not only encourages people to think and explore the idea that less is more, it changes people at their very core. When you talk with your fellow citizens, you experience caring, and you begin to value people more than things. When you talk with people in a convivial and congenial environment, you begin to truly believe that we're all in this together. You begin to truly understand that less is more.

Notes

A Scientific Approach to Voluntary Simplicity

1. The article is based on K. W. Brown and T. Kasser, "Are Psychological and Ecological Well-being Compatible? The Role of Values, Mindfulness, and Lifestyle, in *Social Indicators Research*, 74, 2005, 349–68. The study was supported by the Society for the Psychological Study of Social Issues, the Simplicity Forum and Seeds of Simplicity.

2. See J. B. Schor, *The Overspent American*, New York: Basic Books, 1998; and J. Dominquez and V. Robin, *Your Money or Your Life*, New York: Viking, 1992.

3. When an analysis is referred to as significant, it means that the chances that the result occurred randomly, or by chance, are small (5% or less). All significant effects noted in this study were below this 5% level, and some were substantially below it.

4. Emotions were measured with a scale developed in E. Diener and R. A. Emmons, "The Independence of Positive and Negative Affect," *Journal of Personality and Social Psychology*, 47, 1985, 1105–17. Life Satisfaction was measured with a scale developed in W. Pavot, E. Diener and E. Suh, "The Temporal Satisfaction with Life Scale, *Journal of Personality Assessment*, 70, 1998, 340–54.

5. The behavioral measure was adapted from I. Green-Demers, L. G. Pelletier and S. Menard, "The Impact of Behavioural Difficulty on the Saliency of the Association Between Self-determined Motivation and Environmental Behaviours," *Canadian Journal of Behavioural Science*, 29, 1997, 157–66. The ecological footprint measure was based on R. Dholakia and M. Wackernagel, *The Ecological Footprint Questionnaire*, 1998.

6. The concept of mindfulness and its associations with well-being are described by K. W. Brown and R. M. Ryan, "The Benefits of Being Present: Mindfulness and Its Role in Psychological Well-being," *Journal of Personality and Social Psychology*, 84, 2003, 822–48. More on how mindfulness could influence consumerism can be found in E. L. Rosenberg, "Mindfulness and consumerism," in T. Kasser and A. D. Kanner, eds., *Psychology and Consumer*

Culture: The Struggle for a Good life in a Materialistic World pp. 107–25, Washington, DC: American Psychological Association, 2004.

7. This distinction was first described in T. Kasser and R. M. Ryan, "Further Examining the American Dream: Differential Correlates of Intrinsic and Extrinsic Goals," *Personality and Social Psychology Bulletin*, 22, 1996, 281–88. Later cross-cultural work provides excellent evidence for this distinction: F. M. E. Grouzet, T. Kasser, A. Ahuvia, J. M. Fernandez-Dols, Y. Kim, S. Lau, R. M. Ryan, S. Saunders, P. Schmuck and K. M. Sheldon, "The Structure of Goal Contents Across 15 Cultures," *Journal of Personality and Social Psychology*, 89, 2005, 800–16.

8. See Kasser's *The High Price of Materialism*, Cambridge: MIT Press, 2002; or "Materialism and Its Alternatives," in M. Csikszentmihalyi and I. S. Csikszentmihalyi, eds., *A Life Worth Living: Contributions to Positive Psychology*, pp. 200–14, Oxford: Oxford University Press, 2006.

9. To test these ideas, we used a procedure called Structural Equation Modeling (SEM), which allows researchers to test different pathways through which variables are related to each other. SEM tests show well that the proposed model "fits" the empirical data. Our model fit quite well.

10. D. Elgin, *Voluntary Simplicity* (Revised edition), New York: William Morrow, 1993.

11. Also see M. Burch, *Stepping Lightly: Simplicity for People and the Planet*, Gabriola Island, BC: New Society, 2000.

12. See Kasser, note 8, for a more detailed discussion of these ideas.

Like Corn in the Night: Reclaiming a Sense of Time

1. Henry David Thoreau, *Walden and Resistance to Civil Government*, William Rossi, ed., New York: W.W. Norton, 1992, p. 75.

2. Juliet Schor, "The (Even More) Overworked American," in *Take Back Your Time: Fighting Overwork and Time Poverty in America*, John de Graaf, ed., San Francisco: Berrett-Koehler, 2003, p. 10.

3. William Dougherty and Barbara Carlson, in John de Graaf, "Overscheduled Kids, Underconnected Families," *Take Back Your Time: Fighting Overwork and Time Poverty in America*, John de Graaf, ed., San Francisco: Berrett-Koehler, 2003, p. 41.

4. Tim Kasser, *The High Price of Materialism*, Cambridge: MIT Press, 2002

5. John de Graaf, "Overscheduled Kids, Underconnected Families," *Take Back Your Time: Fighting Overwork and Time Poverty in America*, John de Graaf, ed., San Francisco: Berrett-Koehler, 2003.

Index

economics: based on consumption, 213–216; based on oil, 207–208; and belief in growth, 95–96, 235–236; and community, 208–210; comparison of US and Europe, 236–239, 240–241; and crisis of 2008, 56–57; downshifting, 230–234; and quality of life, 184, 238, 239–240; sustainable *vs.* materialistic, 25, 42–46, 104, 215–216; urban-industrial, 82–83, 136–137; and wealth gap, 57–59

education, 193–197, 198–199, 248, 256–257. *see also* learning

Eliot, T. S., 61

energy conservation: and Carter administration, 13–14; in households, 128, 131; and localization, 210–211; strategy for, 223–225

energy consumption: recent history of, 213–216; strategy for decreasing, 228–234; US v. Europe, 239

energy self-sufficiency, 11

environment (*see also* carbon dioxide emissions; climate change): at community level, 166, 168–169, 177, 178, 195–197, 198; and education, 193–197, 198–199; and green triangle, 99–100; and health problems, 126–128, 131–132; policies for, 217; and rebuilding future communities, 175, 176; and religion, 129–130, 131; and speed, 184, 185–186

equality, 238

Europe/European Union: comparison of economies with US, 237–239, 240–241; and consumerism, 102, 237; and lagom, 101–106; and living in Poland, 109–112, 113–114; and quality of life, 59, 164; and social changes, 43–44

F

family life, 71, 116–120, 145. *see also* social relations

farming: and community-supported agriculture, 99, 178; and connection to nature, 121–125, 192–193; dreaming of, 134–135; as homesteading, 66–69; Nearings' view of, 137–138, 139–140

feminism, 249, 254

finances, personal: changing thinking about, 56–57; coping with decline in, 96, 111; exchanging income for time, 229–234, 237–238; and happiness, 56, 208–209, 246, 252–253; increase of, for wealthy Americans, 236–237; opting for earning less, 183–184; reducing spending, 89–90, 94–95, 99–100; savings rate, 230, 238, 251; and simplicity, 26

Finland, 240–241

food: cost of, 93; and environment, 123; and family meals, 117, 118; and health, 45–46; and killing animals for, 121–123; processing and preparation, 137–138; and saying grace, 30–32; slow food movement, 60, 145, 189–190

About the Editors

CECILE ANDREWS is the author of *Slow is Beautiful: New Visions of Community, Leisure, and Joie de Vivre* as well as *Circle of Simplicity: Return to the Good Life*. She is a founder of the Phinney EcoVillage, a neighborhood project in Seattle building sustainability and community. A former community college administrator, Cecile has her doctorate in education from Stanford University. She now focuses on community education, helping people live simpler, slower, and smaller. See cecileandrews.com and phinneyecovillage.net.

WANDA URBANSKA is the author or co-author of seven books, including *Simple Living; Nothing's Too Small to Make a Difference* and *Moving to a Small Town*. She is host/producer of the nationally syndicated public television series *Simple Living with Wanda Urbanska*, which has produced four broadcast seasons (SimpleLivingTV.net). A graduate of Harvard University, Urbanska has published in the *Washington Post, Los Angeles Times, Chicago Tribune, Mother Earth News*, and *Natural Home*, among others.

If you have enjoyed *Less is More*, you might also enjoy other

Books to Build a New Society

Our books provide positive solutions for people who
want to make a difference. We specialize in:

Sustainable Living ✦ Ecological Design and Planning

Natural Building & Appropriate Technology ✦ New Forestry

Environment and Justice ✦ Conscientious Commerce

Progressive Leadership ✦ Resistance and Community

Nonviolence ✦ Educational and Parenting Resources

New Society Publishers
ENVIRONMENTAL BENEFITS STATEMENT

New Society Publishers has chosen to produce this book on recycled
paper made with 100% post consumer waste, processed chlorine free,
and old growth free.

For every 5,000 books printed, New Society saves the following
resources:[1]

21	Trees
1,929	Pounds of Solid Waste
2,122	Gallons of Water
2,768	Kilowatt Hours of Electricity
3,506	Pounds of Greenhouse Gases
15	Pounds of HAPs, VOCs, and AOX Combined
5	Cubic Yards of Landfill Space

---

[1]Environmental benefits are calculated based on research done by the
Environmental Defense Fund and other members of the Paper Task Force who study
the environmental impacts of the paper industry.

For a full list of NSP's titles, please call 1-800-567-6772 or check out our web site at:

www.newsociety.com

NEW SOCIETY PUBLISHERS